FINDING GOD

through Poetry

FROM FAITH TO FACT

DR. MIKE WILLIAMSON

xulon
PRESS

To Pastor Dylan,

Please share this book with your church. The poems point to Scriptures that ablate.

Blessings

Nate Stilhamson, PhD

FINDING GOD THROUGH POETRY
FROM FAITH TO FACT

The poems in this book attempt to tell the greatest story ever told in the context of End-Times and Jesus' role in them. They express an urgency for being ready for events that are about to take place.

BY

DR. MIKE WILLIAMSON

Table of Contents

Dedication

*T*his book is dedicated to the memory of my good friend the late Jack Scharn, whose poetry was my first source of inspiration. I pray his influence will continue, indefinitely, to impact readers toward a relationship with God through Jesus. Even though Jack's passing has left a hole in my heart, I pray that hole will be filled with many more pages of inspired poetry from our living Savior.

Introduction

$\mathcal{T}$his book declares that we are living in the Final Generation before Jesus Christ returns to rapture His true followers. *It is the same generation He referred to when He said:*

> This generation shall not pass, till all these things be fulfilled. (Matthew 24:34b)

The Bible is unmistakably clear about the literal return of Jesus Christ to "snatch away" His Church. In an instant millions of Christians leave the earth to meet Christ in the clouds.

Jesus said:

> ...so shall also the coming of the Son of man be. Then shall two be in the field; the one shall be taken, and the other left. Two women shall be grinding at the mill; the one shall be taken, and the other left. Watch therefore: for ye know not what hour your Lord doth come. (Matthew 24:39b-42)

Unfortunately, a large majority of the people in the world do not believe the Bible, nor in the God of the Bible, nor in the Deity of His Son, and thus they scoff at the idea of a literal *rapture* of the Church.

According to the Pew Research Center, approximately two-thirds of the population of the world either claim to have no religion or believe in gods other than the God of the Bible.[1]

Also according to Pew, the number of Americans who do not identify with any religion is on a recent growth spurt. One-fifth of the U.S. public and a third of adults under thirty are religiously unaffiliated today, the highest percentages ever in Pew Research Center polling.[2]

If Pew polling is correct, and we have no reason to doubt it, then the majority of the world's population need to rethink their belief about God, and each individual needs to be completely convinced about one of two possibilities:

1. The God of the Bible *does not exist;* there is no reason to fear, because the idea of an afterlife is a myth.
2. The God of the Bible *does exist and it is extremely important to know what He requires in preparation for life after death, and then to comply with His will.*

I am a born-again Christian *and* a behavioral scientist. My faith-based relationship with the God of the Bible provides constant evidence of His existence that is so confirming, it is irrefutable. Multiple millions of Christians throughout history have made the same claim, and millions of others alive today also would concur.

In contrast, non-believers do not have the same *experiential* points of reference. Without those real live experiences they are vulnerable to false teachings.

The Bible says:

> The natural man receives not the things of the Spirit
> of God: for they are foolishness unto him: neither can
> he know them, because they are spiritually discerned.
> (1 Corinthians 2:14)

The Bible also says, in the last days before Christ returns to rapture His Church, false prophets and false teachers will be plentiful, and they will deceive many into believing that God is a myth. The prophecy of the false teachings has been thoroughly fulfilled within the past sixty-five to seventy years, validating the accuracy of its predictions.

In many ways people today are like Doubting Thomas, one of Jesus' Disciples, who had to see and touch the nail prints in His hands and the scar in His side before he could believe in the risen Christ. Like Thomas, the present day doubters, atheists, and God-haters have concluded that faith in God's Word is insufficient proof. They also have deceived themselves into believing that scientific evidence of His reality does not exist.

Richard Dawkins and the late Christopher Hichens are, or were, respectively, representatives of that non-believing segment of the population.

Dawkins stated: "There is no well-demonstrated reason to believe in God,"[3] the God of the Bible. Hitchens parroted Dawkins when he said: "There is no plausible or convincing reason, certainly no evidential one, to believe that there is such an entity."[4] The "entity" he was talking about is God.

I reject the presumptions of Dawkins and Hichens and thousands of others who espouse their false teachings.

Over the years, I have had several experiences that were so remarkable they seemed to me to exceed all possibilities of being accidental happenstances, or mere coincidences. I set out to examine those apparent supernatural events and to mathematically test them against chance as an explanation.

As we proceed, it will become abundantly clear that the words and the experiences we write about were inspired by God. That statement was based on the *fact* that the *manifestations* we originally set out to *test* were supplemented by *eight revelations*. Those revelations also related to issues we either were writing about or directly dealing with at that moment in time. That means God, not chance, is the only tenable explanation.

The difference between "manifestations "and "revelations" was: the *manifestations* referred to *first read* scriptures that took place periodically over a span of fifty years. The *revelations were live,* for the most part.

3

At the outset we were interested in finding an answer to the question: were the historical *manifestations* explainable by chance, or did they have some other tenable explanation?

My Bible contains 1,365 pages and 31,102 verses, reportedly. The investigation was justified by my awareness that over the years there were significant times and issues where God seemed to send a message. The cited verses clearly conveyed messages we needed at the time.

Thus, the original plan was to apply statistical tests to the pool of *manifestations* that were historical, documented in written records. And that was our specific, exclusive objective. We planned to calculate the statistical probability that they were due to chance. At the end of Chapter 2 we report that probability.

The *revelations* turned out to be an unforeseen supplement to the investigation. Each *revelation* was timed to highlight certain scriptures or events. At the time of their occurrence, each was like a real person in the room with a pointer, telling me, *"Pay attention to this one; it is very important!"* Each was relevant to the issue with which we were involved at the time. Their timing allowed us to make the description of the event an integral part of the story being written, thereby, enhancing the topic with *live,* objective, confirming evidence, as you shall see.

Both the *manifestations* and the *revelations* were so surreal, they had visceral effects—they caused goosebumps, a tingling sensation throughout my body, and even trembling. Each was an unforgettable experience, as if I was in the presence of the Living God.

As a scientist, I understand that the experiences in this book were anecdotal and not reproducible by independent investigators. Thus, despite their scintillating and fascinating reality, that deficit means they do not meet all of the *necessary* and *sufficient* conditions to qualify as scientific evidence.

Nevertheless, the evidence we describe here is remarkable to say the least. So, as the saying goes: "we report, you decide."

Regardless of what you decide about the veracity of our anecdotal experiences, they inspired additional research. One chapter in this book, titled *Prophecies Real Time,* Chapter 23, does contain reproducible facts and qualifies as a scientific study.

The book to follow, *Finding God through Science, From Fact to Faith,* is based on several categories of reproducible findings.

Bible prophecies are *faith-based* expectations until they are fulfilled. When they actually take place as scheduled, they transition into *facts* that can be tabulated and tested mathematically for validity, and *they are* reproducible by independent investigators. Thus, unlike anecdotal observations, fulfilled prophecies meet the *necessary* and *sufficient* conditions to be examined scientifically.

Thus, this book, *Finding God through Poetry, From Faith to Fact,* is primarily about the *experiential* bases of the existence of God. Its sequel to follow, *Finding God through Science, From Fact to Faith,* is primarily about scientific tests of prophetic fulfillments that confirm the existence of God, based on reproducible, factual evidence.

In 1949 Fulton Oursler published *The Greatest Story Ever Told.*[5] The book retold the story of Jesus Christ, from His birth through to His Resurrection. It became a classic; it was reprinted scores of times; it was read by millions of people; it remains today as one of the most successful bestsellers of all time.[6]

Fast forward sixty-five years from the first publication of Oursler's book to another captivating story about God. On Christmas Day, 2014, Eric Metaxas published an article in the *Wall Street Journal,* under the title, *"Science Increasingly Makes the Case for God".*[7]

Less than two weeks after his post, in an interview on Fox News, Metaxas stated, the article had more readers than any article published in the history of the online version of *The Journal.*[8]

Obviously, interest in Christ and God is not dead, despite the claims by some that these two very real Beings are simply myths and do not exist.

Thus, there now are two new "greatest stories" to be told.

1. The story of Jesus Christ, whose own words identify the present generation as one in which He returns in the clouds to redeem His followers. That means most people now living will still be living to experience the instant disappearance of millions of people from the earth.
2. The story of prophetic fulfillments that scientifically prove the existence of God, the God of the Bible. Some of those

prophecies, made thousands of years ago, identify the precise date of their fulfillment, which we witnessed in our lifetime. Others occurred earlier and are recorded history. Still others are predicted to occur on dates already set in the near future, *as prophesied*. The facts are irrefutable!

Together the two stories are so profound they should be breaking news, published in every language and broadcast on all media with worldwide distribution. As you shall see, we have reason to believe that too will happen.

Important Relevant Details

We were motivated to write the present book for three important reasons:

1. We wanted to help people understand who God is and what He offers humanity, including a personal relationship with His Son, Jesus Christ, which is by faith the *necessary* and *sufficient* path to Heaven and eternal life.
2. We wanted to examine personal experiences we knew about prior to writing that we believed would help confirm the existence of God. Many false-teachers continue to espouse the presumption that God does not exist and that there is no way for science to prove He does exist. The reality of experiences reported here contradict those deceptive false teachings.
3. We wanted to alert people to the signs of the times. The Bible contains an abundance of references that identify the present generation as the generation in which Jesus Christ will return to *rapture* the Church and set up His millennial reign as a Righteous King.

To Christian readers: we believe many experiences reported here will resonate with you. As you know, the very conversion experience is *faith-based* and also *life-changing,* the effects of which are immediately observable in a person's lifestyle. In other words, observable differences follow a Believer's born-again experience that are overtly recognizable in word, thought, and behavior. When that happens, *faith* literally becomes *fact*.

For true followers of Christ, God's Word becomes a source of spiritually wholesome principles to live by that promote truth, light, love, and life and produce knowable fruit. The concurrence of those common kinds of experiences, yours and ours, should be encouraging to you and strengthen your faith, and provide valid evidence to the world that God exists.

Even the world can know you by your good fruit, if you indeed are producing the right fruit.

> *Ye shall know them by their fruits.* Do men gather grapes of thorns, or figs of thistles? Even so every good tree bringeth forth good fruit; but a corrupt tree bringeth forth evil fruit. A good tree cannot bring forth evil fruit, neither can a corrupt tree bring forth good fruit. Every tree that bringeth not forth good fruit is hewn down, and cast into the fire. Wherefore by their fruits ye shall know them. (Matthew 7:16-20)

To non-Christians: the most important decision you will ever make in life is the one that determines your eternal destiny! The fact is, you choose your destiny. Which will it be, Heaven or Hell?

Anything we can do to make you aware of the destructive effects of sin in your life so you confront its reality and seek God's forgiveness, we want to accomplish, in the kindest and most loving way possible.

If you are a non-believer, we plead with you to open your heart to God. Until you sincerely desire to know God and earnestly seek Him, you will continue to be spiritually blind. We hope and pray the evidence in this book and its sequel will cause your eyes to be opened and your heart to be receptive.

There is a God-shaped void in every person's soul, until God is invited to fill it. We believe many people sense their need for God and are actively searching for Him. You may be one of them. Anyone whom the Holy Spirit convicts can have that pervasive emptiness — that unquenchable thirst — satisfied. This book provides the steps.

God's Gift of Eternal Life

A personal, life-changing relationship with God through His Son, Jesus, is not complicated. It simply requires a sincere belief that Jesus is God's Son, and He paid for the sins of every human being by His death on the Cross and His subsequent resurrection.

Then, when the individual humbly confesses their sins, asks for forgiveness, and sincerely believes they are forgiven, they possess the gift of eternal life. In fact, the chapters titled *Jesus' Gift* and *My Confession,* provide specific steps and a prayer you can pray so your personal relationship with God, through Christ, becomes a reality.

The Poetry is a Pointer

Much of the message of the book is conveyed through poetry. Poetry has the ability to arouse curiosity, communicate succinctly, paint pictures in the mind, and be intellectually and emotionally persuasive. The poetic verses point to authoritative references on adjacent pages, including:

1. Scripture, which must be received, believed, and acted upon as intended, to experience its relevance, power, and benefits.
2. Facts contributed by respected scientists and Bible scholars, along with personal *manifestations* and *live revelations* of God's direct interventions, tested mathematically against chance as an explanation.

Road to a Perfect Heart

The chapter titled *Road to a Perfect Heart,* cites numerous, personal experiences that cannot be explained as random accidents or due to chance. They can only be explained as *caused* by the direct intervention of the Living God.

However, without question, the most fascinating feature of the chapter is eight supernatural events that occurred in direct relation to particular Bible verses we were writing about.

Clearly, God had an important purpose for manifesting Himself in those *live revelations*. One possible purpose may be to alert Christians everywhere about the urgency of the times in which we live.

We are living in the generation when "the book is open again." In the sixth century BC, God told His prophet Daniel to "seal up the book until the time of the end."

To Daniel, God said:

> But thou, O Daniel, shut up the words, and *seal the book, even to the time of the end:* many shall run to and fro, and knowledge shall be increased. (Daniel 12:4, emphasis mine)

We know the "time of the end" is near through many facts, two of which are the facts that transportation and knowledge, referenced in Daniel 12:4, have exploded in the last seventy years like no other time in human history. Many other end-time events are coming into view on the horizon and others are being reported in the daily news.

Then, in the first century AD, God told His prophet, John, who was exiled on the Isle of Patmos, to "not seal" events that are to occur as "the end" approaches.

To John, He said:

> *Seal not* the sayings of the prophecy of this book: for the time is at hand. He that is unjust, let him be unjust still: and he which is filthy, let him be filthy still: and he that is righteous, let him be righteous still: and he that is holy, let him be holy still. And, behold, I come quickly; and my reward is with me, to give every man according as his work shall be. (Revelation 22:10-12)

The verses just cited seem to identify a time when evil will be so rampant that God removes His restraining hand and allows man to do what he will, such that, God is *no longer considered* in mankind's decisions and affairs. Is civilization already at that point in its "progress"? There are many reasons to believe our nation, in fact, nations on a global scale have already crossed that line.

9

Regardless, the time is short! Whatever people intend to do to prepare themselves or to share the Gospel of Christ must be done quickly. Christians around the world need to wake up, clean up (get ready), and look up: "your redemption is near (imminent)"! (Luke 21:28)

Our prayer is that every reader will give serious thought to the book's content and allow it to have an edifying, even life-changing effect, and for readers who are searching for God, an eternal life-changing effect.

If you find spiritual light to walk in through this book, it is quite possible members of your family, your friends, or even your employees, if you have them, might have a similar experience, so please share it.

Also, you are invited to read our blogs at *Prophecies to Watch*, found on our website at www.mikewilliamsonllc.com. At the website, we also make available materials and opportunities that are intended to inspire.

God bless!

Chapter 1

My Call

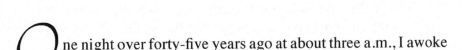

O ne night over forty-five years ago at about three a.m., I awoke
with a very real sense of the presence of someone in the room.
Strange! Very strange!

I couldn't sleep.

I got up . . . went into the family room . . . switched on the light
over the desk . . . looked around.

Nothing!

But, whoever or whatever that "presence" was, he or she or it
was still there.

I waited, as if expecting to hear the Presence speak audibly.

Silence.

Instantly, my thoughts raced to recall the Bible story of Samuel.
He too was awakened, actually heard an audible voice, and felt a
Presence, perhaps the same One I felt.

My response to the situation was, "Lord, are you trying to tell
me something?"

At that particular time, I had finished all of my course work at the
University of Southern California (USC) and was scheduled to make
an oral defense of my dissertation for the PhD degree.

My professional career was about to begin, full-time, with undi-
vided attention.

Just as Samuel received his call, this was my moment. This
was *My Call!*

My Living Bible was on the desk. I looked at it. Could it be that God had a message for me? I reached down, pulled it under the light, opened it, and began to read.

These were *the first words* I read:

> Sing to the Lord, all the earth! Sing of his glorious name! Tell the world how wonderful he is. How awe-inspiring are your deeds, O God! How great your power! (Psalm 66:1-2, TLB[9])

The verses were from the Bible, God's Word. That night, the Word was specifically for me. I call this my *first manifestation*.

Each of the first three sentences in the scripture quoted above begins with an action word, a verb. For the subject, I inserted the pronoun, "You".

I heard a voice that night, loud and clear:

"Mike! You sing to the Lord! You sing of his glorious name! You tell the world how wonderful He is. This is *My Call* to you!"

The Presence was so real, there was absolutely no doubt in my mind; "*My Call*" was from the invisible, but Living God.

Immediately, I said, "Yes, Lord, I accept! I will!"

***

More than thirty years earlier, on an equally significant occasion, I had given a similar response to another call of God.

This story really began on *that* day.

It happened on a Sunday morning in a small protestant church in Burns, Oregon.

I was only eight years old, but on that day I made the most important and wisest decision of my life.

Mrs. Long, the mother of one of my best friends, asked if I would like to invite Jesus into my heart. Without a moment's hesitation, I said, "Yes!"

She led me to the altar at the front of the church where I got on my knees and prayed and cried and confessed my many sins. In a few minutes, I believed that I was forgiven.

As the awareness of what happened dawned, a sense of peace replaced the tears, flooding me with waves of joy. It was as if a great weight had been lifted off my shoulders. It was *real!* It was *right!* It was *glorious!*

My parents were strong Christians. They encouraged me, and soon I was memorizing verses, then chapters in the Bible.

That practice continues to the present day.

In fact, God expects all of His children to know His Word. He says:

> [You] study to shew thyself approved unto God, a workman that needeth not to be ashamed, rightly dividing the word of truth. (2 Timothy 2:15)

> Thy Word have I hid in my heart that I might not sin against Thee. (Psalm 119:11)

> Thy word is a lamp unto my feet and a light unto my path. (Psalm 119:105)

> Jesus said to the people, I am the Light of the world. So if you follow me, you won't be stumbling through the darkness, for living light will flood your path. (1 Peter 8:12, TLB)

> [You] let your light so shine before men, that they may see your good works, and glorify your Father which is in heaven. (Matthew 5:16)

***

To stay on point with the thesis of the book, we must fast-forward to the family room again to finish reading the scripture that constituted, *My Call*, then take a close look at the verses and evaluate evidence of their fulfillment, or lack thereof.

Let's begin by looking at the most relevant verses.

But wait! We have a problem!

The very first verse says: "Sing…." "Tell…." *My Call* was from God. He was saying: "You sing…." "You tell…."

The reality then and now: I do not know music; I play no musical instrument; I am not a vocalist; at the time, I rarely spoke publicly.

While I was confident *My Call,* by God, was for a purpose, I certainly had objective reasons to question being required to tell the world much of anything, and to do that through any form of music was even more unrealistic.

Nevertheless, I already had agreed, audibly, to do what God was asking of me. In effect, I had made a promise to God. I had given Him my word without realizing I was not even a candidate for keeping it in its literal fulfillment.

So, what to do? Hmmm!

Well, no reason to panic!

Typically, in situations like that, I focus my thoughts on scripture already "written on my heart."

Verses like these pop into my head:

> Trust in the Lord with all thine heart; and lean not unto thine own understanding. In all thy ways acknowledge him, and he shall direct thy paths. (Proverbs 3:5-6)

> [Jesus said:] With men this is impossible; but with God all things are possible. (Matthew 19:26)

> I can do all things through Christ who strengthens me. (Philippians 4:13)

> If God be for us, who can be against us? (Romans 8:31)

> My grace is sufficient for thee: for my strength is made perfect in weakness. Most gladly therefore will I rather glory in my infirmities, that the power of Christ may rest upon me. (2 Corinthians 12:9)

> I pray that you will begin to understand how incredibly great his power is to help those who believe him.

It is that same mighty power that raised Christ from
the dead and seated him in the place of honor at God's
right hand in heaven. (Ephesians 1:19-20, TLB)

I do not have the vocabulary, nor do I have the writing skills to
adequately convey the value, the benefits, or the level of encourage-
ment verses like those just cited provide when difficult, challenging
circumstances arise.

Before we go on, let me ask you: Do you have challenges that
seem like mountains you can't get over, around, or through—impos-
sible circumstances?

Be encouraged!

> Got any rivers you think are uncrossable?
> Got any mountains you can't tunnel through?
> God specializes in things thought impossible;
> He can do what no other power can do.

Psalm 66 continues where we left off:

Let everyone bless God and sing his praises; for he
holds our lives in his hands, and he holds our feet to
the path. You have purified us with fire, O Lord, like
silver in a crucible. You captured us in your net and
laid great burdens on our backs. You sent troops to
ride across our broken bodies. We went through fire
and flood. But in the end, you brought us into wealth
and great abundance. (Psalm 66:8-12, TLB[9])

Now I have come to your Temple with burnt offerings
to pay my vows. For when I was in trouble, I prom-
ised you many offerings. That is why I am bringing
you these fat male goats, rams, and calves. The
smoke of their sacrifice shall rise before you. (Psalm
66:13-15, TLB)

Come and hear, all of you who reverence the Lord, and I will tell you what he did for me: For I cried to him for help with praises ready on my tongue. He would not have listened if I had not confessed my sins. But he listened! He heard my prayer! He paid attention to it! (Psalm 66:16-19)

Blessed be God, who didn't turn away when I was praying and didn't refuse me his kindness and love. (Psalm 66:20, TLB)

Then Psalm 67 says:

O God, in mercy bless us; let your face beam with joy as you look down at us. Send us around the world with the news of your saving power and your eternal plan for all mankind. (Psalm 67:1-2, TLB)

For the earth has yielded abundant harvests. God, even our own God, will bless us. And peoples from remotest lands will worship him. (Psalm 67:6-7, TLB)

It was a phenomenal, life-changing moment! The God of the universe had revealed Himself to me in a personal way that was absolutely awesome!

The first level of impact was powerful and immediate. I became obsessed with the verses in *My Call*. In fact, I memorized both chapters and have quoted them dozens of times since.

At the time, I looked into the future, with faith-based hope and expectation. That is what unfulfilled promises and prophecies are — faith-based hopes and expectations.

As the weeks and months and years went by, my faith grew in the conviction that God had a plan that "in the end" would be very significant. I was thoroughly convinced of that!

Now, forty-five years later, I have the benefit of reviewing the journey and connecting the dots of experience with the prophecies embedded in *My Call*, many of which have become fulfilled facts.

However, as *My Call* implied, and as we shall see, before "the end" would come, I would have a very heavy cross to bear.

The Children of Israel wandered in the desert for forty years before they entered the Promised Land. Similarly, it was slightly more than forty years from the date of *My Call,* in 1970, to the date I received a letter scheduling a hearing for bankruptcy. That letter came on my eightieth birthday. A coincidence? I don't think so!

I had hit a wall! The bankruptcy wall was humanly impossible to move, climb over, circumvent, or tunnel through. I had come to *the end* of myself.

I had one alternative. I turned to God in prayer, in earnest! He heard and answered!

Immediately, a Bible verse appeared in my mind's eye, like reading a teleprompter. That verse also became an obsession:

> Seek ye first the kingdom of God, and his righteousness; and all these things shall be added unto you. (Matthew 6:33)

I credit this experience as my *second manifestation.*

A few days later, as I was praying, without flashing lights, or an earthquake, or even any special sense of Presence, the words of my prayer began to rhyme and the rhyme had meter.

In about three hours, real time, with many fever-pitched moments trying to capture the inspirational poetry that was streaming into my head, a beautiful poem was finished.

It was my first, ever, *The Jesus Way*, Chapters 29 and 30.

Within literally hours of the notice of bankruptcy, with no sign, vision, dream, or other sensory indicator, the ability to "sing of His glorious name," and "tell the world how wonderful He is," became a possibility!

This in fact was my *first revelation*, although I did not recognize it as such, at the time.

Prior to my eightieth birthday, I had not studied poetry and never had much of an interest it. Now at eighty-four, I have written two books and an audiobook that introduce two, updated, new "greatest stories ever told": 1) the story of Jesus as Redeemer, soon to *rapture*

His followers from the earth; 2) scientific proof of the existence of God, the God of the Bible.

Get this!

Several people have indicated they want to write music for some of the poems; in fact, they are working on it as this is being written.

There is more!

We mentioned, earlier, Eric Metaxas' experience of history-making interest in his article in the *Wall Street Journal* on Christmas Day, 2014, *"Science Increasingly Makes the Case for God."* At the time of Eric's interview that publicly disclosed his experience, I was getting close to completing the second book with content that does exactly what the article implied.

That content detailed several sets of objectively obtained, scientifically-tested facts that overwhelmingly identified God as their source, such that, I gave the book the title, *Finding God through Science, From Fact to Faith.*

There is more, still!

On February 5, 2015, a hacker destroyed the operating systems on both of my computers. That delayed the completion and publication of both books by at least six weeks.

I felt abandoned! I did not understand!

Yet, the Bible says:

> But they that wait upon the Lord shall renew their strength. They shall mount up with wings like eagles; they shall run and not be weary; they shall walk and not faint. (Isaiah 40:31)

Since I am not very technically skilled, I use licensed technicians, based in India as consultants. They are very good at helping me get over those kinds of frustrating hurdles.

Nevertheless, I still asked God, audibly: "Why do these things have to happen? How can anything good come from this?"

Still, through His Word, God tells us in firm, reassuring terms:

> And, we know that all things work together for good
> to them that love God, to them who are the called
> according to his purpose. (Romans 8:28)

How many times have you been frustrated, complaining, doubting, and wondering, like me, asking: "Why?"

Well, just as I finished writing about putting music to the lyrics of the poetry, I called my Indian technical support team for help to continue restoring my computers. During a pause in the technician's work, I told him I was writing a book, and I gave him the title.

Immediately, he interrupted with excitement!

He said, "I have a friend over here who is very interested in topics like yours. He even has workshops (seminars), and he will want your book and he will share it!"

Over 250 million Indians speak English.

Is it truly still impossible for me to "Tell the world how wonderful he is"?

I am most happy to tell you that I no longer doubt it will happen, whether through music in a song that goes viral, publicity in one or more public media, an unknown Indian cheerleader, or in some other manner.

The promise that goes with that expectation is:

> For the earth has yielded abundant harvests. God,
> even our own God, will bless us. And peoples from
> remotest lands will worship him. (Psalm 67:6-7, TLB)

The experience was the *second revelation,* and it was *live* right in the middle of my workday.

Meanwhile, at the time of this publication, many of the faith-based promises of Psalms 66 and 67 already have been fulfilled.

Furthermore, forty-five years have passed since *My Call* and nothing has happened to prevent the remaining features of the covenant from being fulfilled. In fact, God has "held my feet to the path" just like He said He would, and I am confident every one of the remaining promises will become realities soon, as well.

19

In the present situation, fulfilled promises and prophecies in *My Call* are strong evidence of God's existence.

Indeed, the night when I got *My Call,* there was only one chance in 31,102 options (the number of verses in the Bible) that I would select *that chapter* and read *that verse first* on *that night,* under *those circumstances,* as I did, in 1970.

In other words, if similar circumstances occurred 30,000 times, *that first verse,* Psalm 66:1, likely would not have been chosen, first, more than once, if at all, by chance.

Furthermore, I know of no other scripture that could have more closely simulated forty-plus years of living than those in the two chapters (Psalms 66 and 67). They correspond very well with what actually took place, or is positioned to take place in the near future.

My faith says the cause was not chance, not random accidental happenstance, and not coincidence. *The cause was God!*

However, as you shall see, the formula eventually would become: $((31102^{-7}) \times (1365^{-1}))$. I will report that result with its interpretation and the conclusion drawn from it at the end of Chapter 2.

In Table 1, below, we extracted key sentences, which were indicators of events to come, some of which are only partially fulfilled or are yet to occur.

You may have had similar experiences for which there seemed to be no solution, like the following:

1. The inability to get a job in spite of an excellent resume.
2. Self-employment with insufficient income.
3. Business partners (cohorts) who benefited from your skills exceedingly more than you did.
4. Business failure, insurmountable debt, the driving desire to reach personal goals (aspirations, dreams) that never materialized.

    The God of all grace, who hath called us unto his eternal glory by Christ Jesus, after that ye have suffered a while, make you perfect, stablish, strengthen, settle you. To him be glory and dominion for ever and ever. Amen. (1 Peter 5:10-11)

Table 1 From the Desert to the Promised Land	
Covenant Promises	**State of Fulfillment**
Sing of his glorious name	Yes through poetic songs
Tell the world how wonderful he is	Yes through books/videos
He holds our lives in his hands	Fulfilled
He holds our feet to the path	Fulfilled
You have purified us with fire, O Lord, like silver in a crucible	A life-long process
You captured us in your net and laid great burdens on our backs	Fulfilled
You sent troops to ride across our broken bodies (through business partners)	Fulfilled
We went through fire and flood (figuratively speaking)	Fulfilled
In the end, you brought us into wealth and great abundance (to be used to build God's Kingdom)	Expected
I have come to your Temple with burnt offerings to pay my vows	Being fulfilled
Come and hear, all who reverence the Lord, and I will tell you what he did for me	Being fulfilled
Send us around the world with the news of your saving power and your eternal plan for all mankind	Expected
For the earth has yielded abundant harvests. Peoples from remotest lands will worship him	Expected

I believe Presence, introduced here and felt many, many times throughout my life, is God, in the Person of the Holy Spirit.

That statement will become an experiential fact at very unlikely times, as we progress through to the end.

> And your ears shall hear a word behind you, saying,
> this is the way, walk you in it, when you turn to the
> right hand, and when you turn to the left. (Isaiah 30:21)

My major for the PhD degree was research design and statistics. Those tools provide the skills required to test evidence, mathematically, for its validity (truthfulness) based on numbers. Over the years, God's method of speaking to me has been through numbers, as in statistical probabilities.

However, God is not limited in how and when or by what means He makes Himself known to people. He has an unlimited number of ways to reveal Himself. So, be prepared for experiences that are most appropriate for you to see, or hear, or in some other way know that God is their source.

Nevertheless, the event that night, the night of *My Call,* was unmistakably real. For me it was God, the Creator and Master of the universe, mysteriously defined as three persons in one: Father, Son, and Holy Spirit. He is Truth, Light, Love, and Life in the purest sense. He is the Great I Am!

While God is the Master of the universe and in full control of it, He also has a plan for every one of His creatures, like you and me. I call it the *Master's Perfect Plan.*

We are a favored generation. We have nearly instant access to information on a global scale. We have the ability to connect the dots between live events anywhere in the world with Bible prophecies predicted to be fulfilled in this generation.

Based on personal research and that done by other scientists and scholars, the evidence is extremely strong that most people now living will still be living when Christ comes to rapture the Church, His true followers.

As prophesied, conditions in the world toward the end of the final generation predict times of trouble. For example, we believe we are now living in the time of "the beginning of sorrows."

> And ye shall hear of wars and rumors of wars: see that ye be not troubled: for all these things must come to pass, but the end is not yet. For nation shall rise against nation, and kingdom against kingdom: and there shall be famines, and pestilences, and earth-quakes, in divers places. *All these are the beginning of sorrows.* (Matthew 8:6-8)

Whereas, God reveals Himself to the world through fulfilled Bible prophecies, as is occurring now in end-time events that make the news, He also reveals Himself to individuals by keeping promises He makes to them. In both situations, what starts out as faith-based expectations, become observable facts. Facts can be quantified. They are the *necessary* and *sufficient* ingredients for testing hypotheses and coming to definitive conclusions, either in support of the hypothesis, or in rejection of it.

While the story of my life, being presented here, began with my acceptance of Jesus as Savior at eight years of age, it climaxed over seventy-five years later with two books of poems, which have unlimited possibilities for singing and telling the story of Jesus to the world.

On the one hand, it is a story filled with struggles, disappointments, and failures—mostly from bad decisions on my part—and many tears.

On the other hand, it is a story of God's patience, mercy, faithfulness, and loving disciplines that purged and perfected the heart of one of His children. While it includes *My Call* and forty years of life in the desert, that desert experience was also my *Road to a Perfect Heart* (Chapter 2).

> For the eyes of the Lord search back and forth across the whole earth, *looking for people whose hearts are perfect toward him,* so that he can show his great power in helping them. (2 Chronicles 16:9, TLB)

Over the years, I have taken three questionnaires that purported to measure spiritual gifts. In all three assessments, I got the highest score possible for the gift of faith, not missing a single item in all three assessments. Evangelism is my second strongest gift.

This book validates the accuracy of those assessments.

What does the Bible tell us about spiritual gifts and the gifts of faith and evangelism in particular?

First, spiritual gifts are not talents, nor are they "fruits of the Spirit." Those attributes develop from decisions and practices controlled by each individual.

Spiritual gifts are given by God, manifested in measures that exceed that of other individuals not similarly blessed. That is true of all spiritual gifts; it is not exclusively true for gifts of faith and/ or evangelism.

With regard to the spiritual gift of faith, it refers to a God-given vision for purposes that are beyond human capabilities. Yet that vision is achievable through the individual's belief that God is their source and He will do through them far more than they would be able to do in the absence of the gift.

The gift of evangelism is the unique, God-given ability to share the good news of the Gospel, boldly empowered by the Holy Spirit. That gift allows the evangelist to have a level of discernment that engages people in conversation in ways that often lead to opportunities to present the Gospel effectively.

Come walk with me so you can bear witness of my *faith-gift* being translated into *facts* in ways that could only be achieved by an ever-present, all-knowing, all-powerful, yet intimately personal God. It will be a fascinating journey, I promise.

> I pray that you will begin to understand how incredibly great his power is to help those who believe him. It is that same mighty power that raised Christ from the dead and seated him in the place of honor at God's right hand in heaven. (Ephesians 1:19:20, TLB)

For the earth has yielded abundant harvests. God,
even our own God, will bless us. And peoples from
remotest lands will worship him. (Psalm 67:6-7, TLB)

My Call and the promises that have been translated into facts,
now, "in the end," can only be described as glorious fulfillments!

Chapter 2

Road to a Perfect Heart

Forty Years in the Desert

*A*s I mentioned, when I got *My Call*, described in Chapter 1, it was at the same time I started my professional career. In a few months, I would be forty years of age.

Before I got my PhD at the University of Southern California (USC), I earned a Master's degree in psychometrics. My Master's thesis was awarded Thesis of the Year by the USC Alumni Association.

While working on the two graduate degrees, I also was on the staff at Children's Hospital of Los Angeles (CHLA), School of Medicine.

At CHLA I directed a statewide screening program for the identification of children with a genetic disorder called phenylketonuria (PKU). That project ultimately led to the enactment of legislation that activated blood testing of newborns for genetic disorders.

The project also opened the door for conducting a collaborative study of the treatment of PKU children—a study I was asked to design.

When I got my PhD, I was appointed to the USC Faculty as an Assistant Clinical Professor. Other positions included Chief Biostatistician and Co-investigator of the PKU Collaborative Study.

The Collaborative Study examined a hypothesis by Professor Horst Bickel, MD at the University of Heidelberg. At the end of the study and sixteen years (1964-1980) of carefully controlled diets of these children, the evidence supported the conclusion: "Proper treatment is completely effective in protecting the normal development of the brain in PKU children."

Untreated PKU children had intelligence quotients (IQs) of 30, average, while properly treated PKU children had an average IQ of 100, the same average as their non-PKU siblings—a 70 IQ point benefit from treatment.

Several publications from the study can be found by Google, searching key words, "PKU, Williamson, Koch, Bessman, Dobson, Acosta, Bickle, aspartame, phenylalanine".

On November 17, 1979, at forty-nine years of age, and by then an Associate Clinical Professor, I picked up my last full-time paycheck from USC.

I had decided to become an entrepreneur, although I continued to be a research and statistical consultant, retaining my academic title for another fifteen years.

I wanted to have my own business. I wanted to be my own boss. *My Call* also was still fresh in my mind, making me restless.

I remember, as if it was yesterday, while I was on my way home to Bradbury, California, a small community a few miles east of Pasadena, I had an interesting encounter with the Lord.

As I transitioned from the Glendale freeway to the 134 freeway, I began to talk to the Lord, aloud.

I said, "Lord, I've closed one chapter in the book of my life and am opening another one."

I continued the "conversation," expressing my desires like this:

I'd like to have a business (I had one in mind, to be defined later).

> I want the business to pay the bills so I will be responsible to provide for my family. (The family consisted of my wife, Jan, and four children, ages ten through seventeen, at the time.)

> I'd like to become sufficiently independent so I can have a ministry, one where my true treasures will be laid up in Heaven, which is God's desire for every Christian.

I'd like to work with Christians.

Immediately, my mind's-eye teleprompter turned on!

I didn't know the verse verbatim, but parts of it kept appearing in my head and I heard it ringing in my ears. That continued, over and over again, like an obsession. I tried to quote it several times, audibly.

What I saw, visibly, went something like this:

> All you who are thirsty, come and drink. Or, O, Ye who are thirsty, come and drink. Or, ye who are thirsty, come and drink.

Over and over!

I doubt if I had ever intentionally memorized that verse, and certainly I did not know where it was located in the Bible.

By the time I went to bed that night, the obsessive repetitions had subsided. As was my habit, I always read a scripture before turning out the light. It was my time of personal devotions.

Unconsciously, I opened the Bible, not expecting anything unusual. *There it was! That verse!* The same one I had been obsessed with throughout the evening. This time there was no ambiguity about the wording. This time the truth was staring me in the face.

The *first words* I read that night were:

> Say there! Is anyone thirsty? Come and drink—even if you have no money! Come, take your choice of wine and milk—it's all free. (Isaiah 55:1, TLB)

Goosebumps rose on my arms; the hair stood up. I felt a burning sensation in the back of my neck. Again I felt Presence in the bedroom, exactly the way I had felt Him in that same bedroom almost ten years earlier.

I kept reading.

A few verses later, Presence illuminated the verse He wanted me to see. It was so prominent; it stood out like a blinking neon light.

I am ready to make an everlasting covenant with you, to give you all the unfailing mercies and love that I had for King David. He proved my power by conquering foreign nations. You also will command the nations, and they will come running to obey, not because of your own power or virtue, but because I, the Lord your God, have glorified you. (Isaiah 55:3a-5, emphasis mine)

This was the *third manifestation.*

***

Time out!

I must interrupt this writing and tell you what just happened today, minutes ago—February 18th, 2015.

Except for the miracle of my conversion experience as an eight-year old boy, I just experienced the most dramatic *revelation* of the supernatural in my life!

At the very moment I finished writing the previous verses from Isaiah 55, the doorbell rang. Immediately, I got up and went to the door, eight steps away from my office desk.

No one was there, and no one was in the long hall in either direction from the door.

"Strange! Very strange!"

Do you remember I used the same words to describe the experience the night of *My Call?*

I returned to my desk and sat down, thinking someone was trying to have a little fun with me, although I couldn't imagine either of the single, elderly, neighbor ladies across the hall doing that.

I just touched the keyboard, and the doorbell rang again. I dashed to the door and drew it open.

Nothing! No one! The hall was empty as well.

Instantly, the question popped into my head: "Lord, are you trying to tell me something?"

This time I didn't return to my desk. I closed the door, bowed my head and prayed. "Lord, if you are trying to get through to me, help me get what you want to say."

I barely got the words out of my mouth and the doorbell rang again. I looked through the peephole while it was still ringing.

For the third time, no one was there!

I waited! It stopped for a second, maybe two, maybe three. Then it started again. Ring! Ring! Ring! Pause. Ring! Ring! Ring! Pause.

That pattern continued. By that time, my whole body was tingling! I was trembling.

Presence was in the room!

The only thing left to do was to go to the potential messenger, my Living Bible, to test if this was, or was not, God trying to get through to me.

I hesitated, at first. I did not want to be disappointed.

I picked up the Bible and opened it. Immediately the bell stopped ringing!

My eyes focused on a verse in the middle of a chapter.

Before I even attempt to make sense of it, I am recording it here exactly as the event occurred. I will seek the Lord's help in trying to understand what it means, later.

Now, today, February 18th, 2015, these were *the first words I read*. God was speaking to the prophet, Nathan, telling him what to say to David.

> Now go and give this message to David from the Lord
> of heaven: I chose you to be the leader of my people
> Israel when you were a mere shepherd, tending your
> sheep in the pastureland. I have been with you wher-
> ever you have gone and have destroyed your enemies.
> And I will make your name greater yet, so that you
> will be one of the most famous men in the world! I
> have selected a homeland for my people from which
> they will never have to move. (2 Samuel 7:8-11a)

If the doorbell had not rung on its own accord, without a live human being punching the button, or if it had continued to ring after

I got my Bible, or if the verse had been completely unrelated to the topic at hand (Isaiah 55:3a-5, TLB), I likely would have found some excuse to explain the ringing and soon would have forgotten the incident.

On the other hand, this book, the one you are reading, was conceived as a medium for conveying to the world the possibility that the God of the Bible is real, that He is all knowing, all powerful, and ever present, always available to intervene in the lives of His children.

Think about it! I had just written the narrative of how God guided me thirty-five years earlier to Isaiah 55, where He was ready to make an everlasting covenant with me, comparing my situation with the life of David — *King David!*

The facts are that God did destroy David's enemies; He did make King David one of the most famous men in the world. Also, more than 2,800 years after his forty years of royal reign, the promise of God to bring the Jews back to their homeland is being fulfilled in our generation.

Indeed, just last week Prime Minister Netanyahu of Israel called for all Jews throughout Europe and the world to return to Israel, a call prompted by murderous attacks on the Jews by Islamic extremists in Paris and Copenhagen.[11]

Another verse shifted my focus to the bottom of the page:

> So Nathan went back to David and told him everything the Lord had said. Then David went into the Tabernacle and sat before the Lord and prayed, 'O Lord God, why have you showered your blessings on such an insignificant person as I am? [I relate to that.]

> And now, in addition to everything else, you speak of giving me an eternal dynasty! Such generosity is far beyond any human standard! O Lord God! What can I say? For you know what I am like! You are doing all these things just because you promised to and because you want to!

How great you are, Lord God! We have never heard
of any other God like you. And there is no other God.
What other nation in all the earth has received such
blessings as Israel, your people? For you have res-
cued your chosen nation in order to bring glory to
your name. (2 Samuel 7:17-23a, TLB)

The first read verse in this scenario was the *fourth manifestation,*
and the ringing doorbell by the invisible hand of the Living God
that called my attention to the verses read was my *third, live, super-
natural revelation.*

What happened today was not wishful thinking, or my imagina-
tion, or a delusion, or a distorted perception, or a hallucination! I am
of sound mind and emotionally stable. I have reported it as truthfully
and as accurately as I am capable of doing.

The probability that I would open the Bible to read *that verse,
first,* and those that followed, under the circumstance, where it con-
nected perfectly with Isaiah 55 was truly remarkable!

The thought that the selection was simply a coincidence is too
remote to be believed, especially since the stimulus for opening the
Bible in the first place was the ringing of the doorbell by the invis-
ible hand of God!

***

Now, let's return to the bedroom to Isaiah 55 and try to connect
the dots between the scriptures read and how God will use them to
magnify Himself in the world.

At the time of the *first manifestation,* in 1970, computers were
still in early development, and the Internet and contemporary elec-
tronic media did not exist. So it was a huge leap of faith to believe
that God was speaking to me directly about an everlasting covenant,
the implementation of which would even register with other nations,
say nothing about getting a response from them.

Yet, the experience was of the Lord. It also was consistent with
promises included in *My Call.* Thus, as I had done on other occasions,

I told the Lord: "If this is your voice alerting me to a time in the future in which you plan to do important things through me, I accept!"

I accepted, even though I knew in my heart their fulfillment was another impossibility from the human standpoint. However, as we shall see, evidence is accruing, such that even this prophecy—"you also will command the nations and they will come running to obey"—could be miraculously feasible.

Time will tell.

Both scriptures, the one at the time of *My Call*, Isaiah 55, and those just cited in 2 Samuel, related to David and his leadership "of my people Israel".

Now, thirty-five years between the *two manifestations*, doors of communication are open unlike any time in all of previous history. The Computer Age brought with it the innovation of the Internet and a host of electronic media with instant access to almost any location in the world. Thus, the opportunities to "command the nations" are within the realm of possibility today much more than they were in 1970.

In fact, there are additional reasons for encouragement in that regard.

At about midpoint in my desert experience, on April 10, 1989, nearly twenty years after the first incident, Presence guided me to the scripture below.

At the time it seemed not to apply. It was such a remote possibility, I simply dated the event and dismissed it as having no relevance to me, personally.

Here are the verses:

> You will tell his people how to find salvation through
> forgiveness of their sins. All this will be because the
> mercy of our God is very tender, and heaven's dawn
> is about to break upon us, to give light to those who sit
> in darkness and death's shadow, [Israel, the Jews] and
> to guide us to the path of peace. (Luke 1:77-79, TLB)

The scripture, of course, is the account of the angel, Gabriel, to Elizabeth and Zacharias, telling them their unborn son, John, would be a forerunner of the first coming of Messiah, Jesus.

Now, 2,000 years have passed and we look forward to the second coming of that same Messiah.

Could it be that somehow, someway, indeed, miraculously, God uses this book to "prepare the way" for many Jews, God's chosen people, to accept Jesus as their Messiah?

I believe, now, it can happen. I pray, *and ask that you pray it to be so*.

***

Whoa! Time out! Again!

This is truly amazing! I have never experienced anything like it.

I had just returned to the sentence above to tweak it so it included the phrase *"and ask that you pray it to be so"*. Prior to that I was working on the end of the chapter, trying to finish it. So the entire time at the diverted location making the tweak was less than a minute, but that brief moment was critical to what happened next.

As I completed the insertion of the phrase, I needed something in another room. I left my desk and went to get it.

As I entered the room, I noticed a paper on the floor. Someone had obviously shoved it under the door—the same door I had opened on the 18th when the doorbell rang.

I picked it up. The page had several scripture verses on it, but the first three verses were at the top of the page and they were *the first verses* I read.

> *The Spirit of the Lord God is upon me; because the Lord hath <u>anointed me</u>* [already underlined] *to preach good tidings unto the meek; he hath sent me to bind up the brokenhearted, to proclaim liberty to the captives, and the opening of the prison to them that are bound;*

To proclaim the acceptable year of the Lord, and the day of vengeance of our God; to comfort all that mourn;

To appoint unto them that mourn in Zion [Jews/Israel], to give unto them beauty for ashes, the oil of joy for mourning, the garment of praise for the spirit of heaviness; that they might be called trees of righteousness, the planting of the Lord that he might be glorified. (Isaiah 61:1-3, emphasis mine).

Shocking! This was the *fifth manifestation* and the *fourth live revelation*!

This *revelation,* like the others, was tied to a scripture — either a scripture I was actually writing about at that moment, or one that was specifically related to the incident.

This event was timed to follow the tweak, which took place in a few seconds. Indeed, the event would have had far less impact if my discovery of the paper on the floor had occurred at any other moment in time.

Yet, as incredible as it may seem, another similar live *revelation* is about to be reported.

Keep reading!

However, before we continue...

The verses here clearly relate to evangelizing throughout the world, with an emphasis on bringing the message of salvation to the Jews.

I am more confident than ever that God is keeping His promise of an "everlasting covenant", and He will find a way that allows the words and impact of this book to "tell the world how wonderful He is."

Obviously, God wanted me to see these verses and to hear His voice, because He went to a lot of trouble to get the message (the verses) to me and to reveal His supernatural ability to do that.

In this *revelation,* I did not feel any special presence of Presence, the Holy Spirit. In fact, in this instance, a Christian lady, a friend and neighbor named Jean, was His chosen messenger.

Didn't I mention earlier that God is not limited in ways to reveal Himself?

With all that has happened, a ministry, even at my age and even to the Jews, no longer seems impossible.

Interestingly, Jan and I had the opportunity to attend a meeting where Joel Rosenberg, a Messianic Jew, was the speaker. He is the author of many books on prophecy. I even met him and had him sign one of his books for me.

Joel now lives in Israel.

For Christian readers, here is another prayer request. Please pray that Joel and I can reconnect and a door will open giving me the opportunity to share the story of Jesus to the Jews in Israel, through personal testimony, prophecy and poetry.

***

We must move on.

Let's continue with more episodes of the desert experience and *Road to a Perfect Heart*.

At USC I had developed a database of 5,000 food items, each broken down into twenty plus nutrients. The business I hoped to establish would expand that database to approximately 20,000 food items and develop computer software that would have many applications in health care, nutrient-related disorders, and in the food service management industry.

In 1981, three cohorts and I co-founded a company called Computrition, Inc. It became one of the leading software companies in foodservice software solutions. It can be accessed through www.computrition.com.

Many startup companies are underfunded and do not pay their founders well. That was the case for the first five years of Computrition's beginnings. Even though my skills were imperative for developing the database (which was essential to all service applications), once the database was completed there was nothing for me to do. I became an extra hand which the company could not afford.

While I held twenty-five percent of the company's stock, the only payment was $1,000 per year, sometimes more, sometimes less, for thousands of hours of hard work.

During the five years with Computrition, we as a family lived on Jan's salary as a nurse, and the small consulting fees I earned at USC. That was not enough to feed, clothe, transport, house, and educate four children. In 1986, I left the company to seek employment elsewhere.

Through a special arrangement with the founder of Professional Dynametrics Programs (PDP), a company with headquarters in Colorado Springs, I became the owner of a franchise.

I used the franchise to develop several information technologies for recruiting, selecting, managing, retaining, and promoting personnel in the workplace.

Those activities also took thousands of hours of time and lots of money—money I did not have.

Debts mounted. The equity in our home in Bradbury, California, had to be tapped for us to survive.

By 1989, the kids were out of the nest and on their own. We sold the home in Bradbury, where they had been raised for the most part over a twenty year time span.

Jan and I moved into a condominium in Arcadia, California, a city that shares borders with Pasadena.

Neither time nor space is sufficient to record the many details of disappointing experiences that seemed to occur daily. I called them primrose paths to dead ends.

Jan was working at a doctor's office in Pasadena, while concurrently getting her real estate license. Real estate was a lucrative vocation at the time, and we were desperately considering any and all avenues that would increase our income.

In one attempt, I sent out 3,000 resumes through a California state employment agency. I got a handful of responses, but zero interviews. The responses subtly suggested I was too old, but most stated I was overqualified.

I had a home-based office where I was working around the clock to develop the information technology, mentioned earlier. The technology applies mathematics to identify job candidates who are predicted, by customized equations, to be "highly successful."

The criteria for "success" relate to reductions in unwanted turnover and improvements in performance by client-selected benchmarks.

In any strategy for selecting new hires, fifty percent of the employees do better than the other fifty percent. With my technologies, seventy to eighty percent of new hires turn out to perform above the fiftieth percentile.

The technologies, with deliverables, are described and are available for perusal at www.mikewilliamsonllc.com.[12]

In the early days I had to make the sale and provide services manually. That meant I had to create the instruments that collected the data, administer them, analyze the date, and create the reports by hand. Nothing was automated.

One day I had a meeting with the vice president of an insurance company that I hoped would result in a sale and long term contract. The meeting went well, and I was very encouraged.

For my devotions that night, I opened my Living Bible and these were the *first words read:*

> But, now note this: From today, this 24th day of the month . . . I will bless you. (Haggai 2:18-19)

I checked the calendar and it was June 24, 1991.

***

I recorded the following in the margins of my Bible: "These verses were the best witness I could have asked for that the Lord is with me."

This was another, first verse read experience, and my *sixth manifestation.*

Well, I did sell my services to the insurance company, which became a big percentage of our income for the next ten years.

Three years later, my technologies were succeeding to the point that I needed to automate them. By then I had a name for the software.

I called it SURE, which was an acronym for Success Using Research Equations.

A friend was a computer programmer, whom I wanted to hire to build a website by which clients could obtain services online. The only thing I lacked was the money to adequately fund the project.

I will never forget it! I felt such urgency for God's help, I began to pray in earnest. In fact, I began to fast and pray, pleading for God's intervention.

After praying for the better part of an hour, I felt Presence nudging me to go to *the messenger* again, The Living Bible.

There was no bookmark or paper clip or any other reason for my Bible to open on a particular page, including the one it opened to. It could have opened on any one of the 1,365 pages, and I could have read any one of the verses on any one of those pages.

Nevertheless! *There it was!*

The page opened at Haggai 2, and I suspect I read verses 18 and 19, *first again*, because I recognized the page, although I do not remember that being a factor.

At any rate, after reading the verses, I looked down at my watch and it was the 24th day of the month.

Yes! Presence was in the room.

Again, goosebumps! Again, I was tingling all over. I uttered the words, spontaneously, "I'm standing on holy ground!"

I was ecstatic! The God of the universe had listened. This was the *seventh manifestation*.

> He heard my prayer! He paid attention to it! Blessed be God, who didn't turn away when I was praying and didn't refuse me his kindness and love. (Psalm 66:19b-20, TLB)

Do you remember those words at the end of Psalm 66 of *My Call?*

I continued to pray. I had the encouragement I asked for, including a promise, but I couldn't do anything about it until I had enough money to put the programmer to work.

I was still praying, earnestly, for forty-five additional minutes, when the phone rang.

I picked up the phone and greeted Dr. Don, who was my wife's former boss.

A few weeks before, perhaps as many as four weeks earlier, Jan had quit her nurse's position and was "farming" for clients in her new real estate job.

Don said, "You know, Mike, there was a fund built up over the years while Jan was working here, and it amounts to $xx,xxx. What do you want me to do with the money?"

Both Jan and I had completely forgotten about that consistent deduction in her pay checks. Don's announcement came as a complete shock. However, the money paid for the programming I needed. Equally as important, it was a direct answer to prayer and a great encouragement to our faith!

Praise be to God!

I count this as the *fifth revelation,* the only one that was in retrospect, not live.

***

Stop!

Today, I am reviewing the manuscript of this book, which I received from Xulon Editorial Staff two days ago. I am making final tweaks before resubmitting it to Xulon Production Team for formatting and printing.

Guess what?

I just glanced at my computer calendar and it is June 24, 2015, the exact date of the *second manifestation!*

Let me reassure you, if I can. This *sixth revelation,* like all the others, was controlled by a living, all-knowing, super-intelligent Being. I did absolutely nothing to bring it about. That may be hard for some to believe—I can even understand that—but I am telling you the absolute truth.

Remember what the verse in Haggai says:

> But now note this: from today, this 24th day of the month . . . I will bless you. (Haggai 2:18-19)

Well, as you shall see, as we pick up the reviewing process again, the Lord did bless following both experiences.

Now, He has just committed Himself to it for the third time.

Before continuing with the earlier story, let me point out some other interesting observations that are exceedingly relevant:

1. While the two earlier *manifestations* were three years apart, the *revelation* today was exactly twenty-four years to the day from June 24, 1991.

2. Certain numbers are important to God, and often multiples of a number also have significance, as well. The number twelve is one of His special numbers, along with three, four, seven, and ten. Obviously, the number twenty-four, when divided by two is twelve . Thus, since twenty-four is a multiple of twelve, my curiosity compels me to discover what the number twelve means in God's numbering system. Let's make that discovery together.

3. Among its many meanings, the number twelve means "authority, signs, and time," where two examples for "authority" are the twelve disciples and the twelve tribes of Israel. One example of twelve that represents "signs" is the twelve stars in the crown of the woman (a constellation, about which I know little) that appears in the Heavens in the last days. In fact, many contemporary scholars of prophecy are excited about this particular sign as a signal of the coming Messiah, as King. For "time" twelve hours in the day, twelve hours in the night, and twelve months in the year are examples.

4. Here is the kicker! The significance of the number twenty-four is: "A priestly blessing to the world".[13]

Does Item four, above, ring a bell?

As you might expect, Psalm 66:1-2 from *My Call* flashed into my head.

41

Sing to the Lord, all the earth! Sing of his glorious name! Tell the world how wonderful he is. How awe-inspiring are your deeds, O God! How great your power! (Psalm 66:1-2, TLB)

Other verses followed with almost equal relevance:

O God, in mercy bless us; let your face beam with joy as you look down at us. Send us around the world with the news of your saving power and your eternal plan for all mankind. (Psalm 67:1-2, TLB)

I am ready to make an everlasting covenant with you, to give you all the unfailing mercies and love that I had for King David. He proved my power by conquering foreign nations. *You also will command the nations, and they will come running to obey, not because of your own power or virtue, but because I, the Lord your God, have glorified you.* (Isaiah 55:3a-5, TLB)

You will tell his people how to find salvation through forgiveness of their sins. All this will be because the mercy of our God is very tender, and heaven's dawn is about to break upon us, to give light to those who sit in darkness and death's shadow, [Israel, the Jews] and to guide us to the path of peace. (Luke 1:77-79, TLB)

For the earth has yielded abundant harvests. God, even our own God, will bless us. And peoples from remotest lands will worship him. (Psalm 67:6-7, TLB)

And the verses listed above do not exhaust all of those contained in promises and *manifestations* cited throughout the book that pertain to, "You tell the world . . .".

Before continuing the review of the manuscript, I feel compelled to say that I am blessed beyond my ability to express it to know in my heart that the very real, Living God is making it possible for me to be instrumental in the spiritual birth of other human beings around the world. What an *honor!* What a *delight!* What a *privilege!*

Lord, I am a long way from being worthy of the job, or even qualified, but I can say with certainty, *I am available!* Yes Lord, do what you will!

I hope you are not confused by the interruption. Let's continue the review of the text as it was originally written if the "Stop!" and God's sixth live *revelation* had not occurred.

***

In fact, the insurance company used the program exclusively as a tool for hiring new employees. After SURE was automated, its usage increased considerably, which meant more income for me.

Over the entire ten year period from 1991 to 2001, the insurance company grew from $500 million in sales to $3.6 billion in sales, a twenty-two percent growth rate, compounded annually.

At a face-to-face meeting with the president, he stated: "We wouldn't hire without it," referring to the SURE technology.

The employment manager also gave SURE at least partial credit for the company's growth. After I had read the ten-year annual report and noted the growth rate, I asked her: "To what do you attribute this growth?"

Her immediate response was: "We hire right."

Clearly, there were many additional reasons for the company's rapid growth besides the people it hired, but the evidence also pointed to a very significant contribution of SURE, as well.

In 1994, Jan and I moved to San Diego. Certain doors of opportunity seemed to be opening. Some of those doors turned out to be good, humanly speaking, while others turned out to be human disasters but spiritual victories. They brought us out of our personal forty years in the desert and into the Promised Land.

The story is a marvelous example of how God intervenes to fulfill His promises and achieve His purposes, and He rarely does it in a straight line. Typically there are twists and turns and hills and valleys and rough roads and smooth roads, and blessings and disappointments and disciplines, even failures. At least that was our experience.

By the late 1990's and early 2000's my company under the PDP franchise, which I called Personnel Solutions, was doing well. I was working from my office in our rented home in San Diego. The technologies were unique and highly effective. The insurance company ordered renewals every few months.

Jan was doing well in real estate.

We were making it.

Another good business transaction occurred. It involved an auto dealership. We applied the SURE technology and by the end of its first year, sales had jumped from 500 units per month to as many as 600 units per month.

Success was attracting attention from possible partners, for whom I had begun to look. It had become obvious to me that I needed help. I had many deficits in my ability to manage a company properly.

I wanted to automate my technologies on a bigger and better website, and I needed better sales and marketing services. In short, I needed help, lots of it.

A long-time friend, who had a good practice in clinical psychology, heard about my business and wanted to see me.

We met!

He liked what he saw and wanted in. He had two friends who seemed to satisfy requirements for marketing, sales, and website development.

We founded a corporation and became feverishly engaged, again, in the pain and hazards of another startup company. The year was 2002.

We all agreed my friend would be President and business manager. I was Chief Technology Officer.

Friendship and trust became the hallmark of our business agreement. Legal counsel was not engaged—a red flag for all readers who start a business with partners, even friends.

Investment capital, of course, was critical. The only significant financial resource I possessed was my stock in Computrition, Inc., which I sold.

In retrospect, the decisions being made, unquestionably, were more my will than God's will. I rationalized that I needed to make things happen in a big way if I was ever to fulfill my dream of financial independence that would allow me to be free enough to have a ministry.

Unconsciously, I behaved as if God needed my help in order for the vision of *My Call* to come true.

Big mistake!

However, God did not stop the proceedings. I was in charge.

Two years passed. By then, our part-time programmer in the corporation had developed a functional website, activating databases for reports which I had written, and graphics for displaying many of the deliverables, also using my customized algorithms.

We were beginning to get clients.

Through a previous client of mine, one I had serviced prior to incorporating, we got a large, ten-year contract. The revenue from that account helped pay some of the bills, but the bills by now exceeded, by far, the $5,000 per month from that source of revenue.

While I was picking up the additional tab, one partner felt his work justified payment first. He was young, recently married, and his work with the corporation was a major portion of his income, even though his wife also worked.

In the early years, we held Annual General Meetings (AGMs) by conference call—distance and shortages of funds prevented face-to-face corporation meetings.

By 2005, we were congregating for AGMs in Vancouver, Canada, the location of the corporate offices. Conference calls were common for discussing website development issues, sales and other day-to-day matters of business.

On the third face-to-face AGM—conflict. Big time!

I returned home in despair, totally defeated. I saw the handwriting on the wall. I could not continue paying company bills while acceding to demands for increases in commissions and revenue paid to the partners, where the clients had been mine before the corporation was founded. By that time, the insurance company renewal sales were also being channeled through the corporation.

The Computrition stock, which amounted to two and a-half six figures, was depleted. I was accruing credit card debt at the rate of $2,000 per month, and I had no way to stop it.

Obviously, I was not being blessed by God, and I had to face up to that fact. I had gotten off track with Him. I was in horrible conflict with my business partners. I was very angry and became increasingly bitter by the day. I lashed out at my partners, in writing, telling them how I felt in no uncertain terms.

That was wrong! It had to stop!

I was convicted in my spirit. I began to agonize over my wrongdoing. Finally, I became very sorry for what had taken place, even though it seemed not to be intentional. I did not deliberately, consciously defy God. It seemed to have just happened, although I do not deny the fact it was my responsibility. Nevertheless, I did not know how to deal with it.

I began to pray and fast and pour out my heavy heart to God. Very few times in my life have I wept with more tears or with more contrition.

Again, verses in *My Call* applied.

First:

> You have purified us with fire, O Lord, like silver in a crucible. You captured us in your net and laid great burdens on our backs. You sent troops to ride across our broken bodies. (Psalm 66:10-11, TLB)

Then:

> He would not have listened if I had not confessed my sins. But he listened! He heard my prayer! He paid attention to it! Blessed be God, who didn't turn away when I was praying and didn't refuse me his kindness and love. (Psalm 66:18-20, TLB)

Presence began to nudge me again. What happened next was God's solution to the mess I had gotten myself into!

God's ways are always best.

He says:

> What a God he is! How perfect in every way! All
> his promises prove true. He is a shield for everyone
> who hides behind him, all those that trust in him.
> (Psalm 18:30)

Intellectually, I knew that verse to be true, but I had not allowed
God to be my shield. The nudging continued, so I opened my Living
Bible, the messenger, in response to that still small voice telling me
Presence had something He wanted me to know: These were the *first
words read* that day, August 12, 2007.

> I will climb my watchtower now and wait to see
> what answer God will give to my complaint. And the
> Lord said to me, "Write my answer on a billboard,
> large and clear, so that anyone can read it at a glance
> and rush to tell the others. But these things I plan
> won't happen right away. Slowly, steadily, surely, the
> time approaches when the vision will be fulfilled. If
> it seems slow, do not despair, for these things will
> surely come to pass. Just be patient! They will not be
> overdue a single day"! (Habakkuk 2:1-3)

What was that?

At the time, it didn't make any sense. I already had "a billboard"
in a website that I had invested hundreds of thousands of dollars in
and I was about to lose, and did lose, as we shall see.

Now, more than seven years later, as I look at the events through
the lens of history, the prophetic messages in this yet another *man-
ifestation* are very possible. In fact, within the week, I have created
a new Website where I plan to build a broadcasting platform from
which I can sell books, ebooks, and CDs and DVDs of songs and
poetry, etc. It is located at www.mikewilliamsonllc.com.

At the time, the *manifestation* represented in the verses at
Habakkuk 2:1-3 seemed out of place and irrelevant to my situation.
Now, they make a lot of sense, and I hope to develop a platform on
the website that helps get the message out and helps fulfill every one
of God's remaining promises.

Even then I knew the Lord had spoken, and that was good enough for me. I was at peace. It also gave me a new expectation, a promise, reinforcing the part of *My Call* that said: "You tell the world how wonderful He is".

So, now I look forward to the fulfillment when "these things will surely come to pass."

Now, back to the termination issue.

After the third corporate AGM when we had the conflict, we never had another face-to-face meeting.

In 2009, I engaged an attorney who was an expert in protecting intellectual property. He extricated me from all business agreements, which allowed the partners to continue to use the technologies, even to the present time, but without my involvement.

I still own all of the original technologies, and following termination I developed three more.

Over the next two years, I made a final attempt to get back into business, but due to underfunding and the inability to automate a website containing the technology that too failed.

Remember what I said earlier:

From the date of *My Call,* it was a little over forty years later, I received a letter, exactly on my 80th birthday scheduling a hearing for bankruptcy. The date was October 28th, 2010. The bankruptcy, in fact, was finalized on November 24th, 2010.

Hmmm! That was date of three earlier 24ths. There is no way chance explains these events! I have to count it as my *seventh revelation*.

Interestingly, the number seven in God's numerology means completion.

The timing of the situation paralleled that of the Children of Israel who completed their forty years in the desert and were ready to cross the Jordan into the Promised Land.

Well, within a week after my eightieth birthday and well before the 24th of November, God inspired me to write *The Jesus Way*.

The Jesus Way was also the way to seek first the kingdom of God, which I am fully committed to doing and which contains the promise, "and all these things (material things) shall be added unto you" (Matthew 6:33).

At the time, Jan and I were forced to downsize, selling furniture and most other possessions of value. In July 2012, we moved to the Portland, Oregon area to be within a few miles of where our son and oldest daughter and their families lived.

By then I had parked the technologies and had ceased trying to monetize their application.

We stored the belongings we still owned, and for a few months lived with our daughter while we looked for a place to live.

My son owned a house in Sun River, east of Bend, Oregon. He allowed us to stay there for six weeks, as well. That is where I was inspired to write a second poem, then a third, and soon I was on my way writing what turned out to be this book.

We found a small, affordable apartment in a very nice city and community south of downtown Portland, called Wilsonville, where we now live, comfortably.

Writing has become a passion.

I also enjoy speaking at churches, universities, and numerous other organizations. Those arrangements can be made through my website at www.mikewilliamsonllc.com.

I plan to use every form of electronic media available to distribute the Word to the world as much as I can as quickly as God allows it. There is no time to waste. The End, as in End of Days, the Tribulation, the Rapture and the Second Coming of Christ are upon us.

With the publication of this book and the second to follow soon, I believe the final verses of God's original Word to me that night of *My Call,* will be fulfilled.

> For the earth has yielded abundant harvests. God, even our own God, will bless us. And peoples from remotest lands will worship him. (Psalm 67:6-7, TLB)

Equally significant was the clear expectation of the other prophetic word.

> Write my answer on "a billboard [or blog, or website, or video] large and clear, so that anyone can read it

at a glance and rush to tell the others". (Habakkuk 2:2b, TLB)

My blog at www.mikewilliamsonllc.com should fulfill that purpose. It is conceivable that sufficient time has passed since this book was published that you can evaluate the factual evidence of the fulfillment of all of the remaining promises. If so, I urge you to check it out!

You can do that by examining the extent to which the following questions have been answered:

Are the two books being used as tools for people to come into a personal relationship with God through His Son Jesus Christ?

How many people are hearing the songs, and seeing the videos, and reading the blogs?

Have the Jews had opportunity to meet the true Messiah through the various media, broadcasting this book or portions of it?

Is there any record of an opportunity for me to have visited Israel to speak to the Jews, personally, about the Messiah, possibly through Joel Rosenberg?

***

Before I close this chapter, I must record an *eighth manifestation*. In order to minimize confusion, I will quote the verses here again that I was reviewing at the time:

You will tell his people how to find salvation through forgiveness of their sins. All this will be because the mercy of our God is very tender, and heaven's dawn is about to break upon us, to give light to those who sit in darkness and death's shadow, [Israel, the Jews] and to guide us to the path of peace. (Luke 1:77-79, TLB)

I had reason to check my Bible for a reference. I opened it to get started for the search. My eyes fell on the following verse, which again was the first verse read:

> You shall do more than restore Israel to me. *I will make you a Light to the nations of the world to bring my salvation to them too.* (Isaiah 49:6b, emphasis mine)

I do not remember ever reading that verse before, and I certainly was not looking for it. Like the others the only explanation, as far as I am concerned is the supernatural ability of the Living God to guide my hands and eyes to that location at that particular time. The timing was just as significant as the identification of the verse. Amazing!

I am fully aware that the eight *manifestations* are all anecdotal, because you must take my word for their occurrence, and they are not reproducible by an independent observer. However, I declare to you, they occurred as described. If you accept that to be the case, then you need to see the statistical probability (p) of their chance occurrence.

$$p = ((31102^{-7}) * (1365^{-1}))$$
$$p = 2.60225E\text{-}35$$
$$p = 0.00000000000000000000000000000000000003.$$

Interpretation: It would take similar conditions repeated a quadrillion quadrillion times for exactly the same verses to be selected first again, as they were in the eight *manifestations*.

All of the *revelations* were spontaneous, one-of-a-kind experiences that have no possibility of being repeated, and by their nature it was impossible to calculate an accurate statistical probability of their reoccurrence.

Conclusion: From our perspective, there is no doubt that both the experiences reported here were orchestrated by an ever-present, all-knowing, all-powerful, Living God. The God of the Bible and the creator of the universe.

You have seen the evidence, now you will have to make a decision that either agrees with ours, or disagrees with it, and do what you will in response to it.

I rest my case.

There are many other scenarios we could have included in the saga of our personal wandering in the desert, all of which would add to the existing pool of objective evidence relative to the existence of God. Perhaps those stories will be told in other books that follow.

Based on my age of eighty-four conditions throughout the world, the phase defined in the relevant scriptures as "in the end" seems to have arrived opening a brief span of time for "the vision to be fulfilled."

I am ready!

The poetry that follows, I believe, is God-inspired. I am the writer; God is the author. If that is true, I am humbled, honored, blessed, and very grateful!

Was the road to a perfect heart through the purifying fires of God's loving disciplines in the crucible of financial losses, unfulfilled personal aspirations, and the humiliating awareness of failure worth it?

Yes! Absolutely!

I have the faith to believe many people will be led into a personal relationship with Christ as a result.

Chapter 3

In the Beginning, God

In the fabric of endless time,
there's a story of God's design.
With a Word He spoke creation;
by His Word He brings salvation.

Think of God's creative mind;
every form of life you'll find,
and for each and every kind,
no two alike in their design.

Imagine a scroll of tapestry
displaying all of history.
Let each fiber in its place
tell a story of his grace.

Then every thread and every hue
paint a picture, His Word is true.
That's how it was when time began,
and now "forever" has no end.

In the beginning God...". (Genesis 1:1a)

That is how the Bible begins, and that is how our story begins, as well.

> In the beginning God created the heaven and the earth. (Genesis 1:1)

> In the beginning was the Word, and the Word was with God, and the Word was God. The same was in the beginning with God. (John 1:1-2)

> All things were made by him; and without him was not anything made that was made. In him was life; and the life was the light of men. (John 1:3-4)

> But as many as received him, to them gave he power to become the sons of God, even to them that believe on his name: (John 1:12)

> And the Word was made flesh, and dwelt among us, (and we beheld his glory, the glory as of the only begotten of the Father,) *full of grace and truth.* (John 1:14)

> Blessed is the man that walketh not in the counsel of the ungodly, nor standeth in the way of sinners, nor sitteth in the seat of the scornful. But his delight is in the law of the Lord and in His law doeth he meditate day and night. And he shall be like a tree planted by the rivers of water that bringeth forth his fruit in his season. His leaf also shall not wither and whatsoever he doeth shall prosper. (Psalm 1:1-3)

> Heaven and earth shall pass away: but my words shall not pass away. (Mark 13:31)

God is ever on His throne;
all our thoughts and deeds are known.
When faith in God is practiced,
there's proof of His existence.

He blesses our obedience
and disciplines our resistance.
He judges our abuses,
does not accept excuses

He's ever present in the world;
He sees history, yet unfurled.
He knows the facts of prophecy;
they're intertwined in tapestry.

He knows the heart of every man.
He knew your heart when it began.
Nothing's hidden from His eyes,
nor is He fooled by some disguise.

I saw also the Lord sitting upon a throne.... Holy, holy, holy, is the Lord of hosts: the whole earth is full of his glory. (Isaiah 6:3b)

You know when I sit or stand. When far away you know my every thought. (Psalm 139:1, TLB)

For we walk by faith, not by sight. (2 Corinthians 5:7).

My son, do not make light of the Lord's discipline, and do not lose heart when he rebukes you, because the Lord disciplines the one he loves, and he chastens everyone he accepts as his son. (Hebrews 12:5b-6, NIV)

If we say that we have no sin, we are only fooling ourselves and refusing to accept the truth. (1 John 1:8)

For since the creation of the world God's invisible qualities—His eternal power and divine nature—have been clearly seen, being understood from what has been made, so that men are without excuse. (Romans 1:20)

And this promise is from God himself, who makes the dead live again and speaks of future events with as much certainty as though they were already past. (Romans 4:17b, TLB)

This is too glorious, too wonderful to believe! I can never be lost to your Spirit! I can never get away from my God! If I go up to heaven, you are there; if I go down to the place of the dead, you are there. If I ride the morning winds to the farthest oceans, even there your hand will guide me, your strength will support me. If I try to hide in the darkness, the night becomes light around me. For even darkness cannot hide from God. (Psalm 139:6-12a, TLB)

O Lord, you have examined my heart and know everything about me. (Psalm 139:1, TLB)

Among the portraits there arrayed,
is my story, by threads displayed.
Your story, too, is known to Him;
it's in the center, woven in.

God sees the hate in ruling edicts;
He sees the deaths in warring conflicts.
That's why we pray: "Thy Kingdom come,"
and here on earth: "Thy will be done".

That's why we yearn for your Dear Son
to come again as glorious King,
to complete the scroll of tapestry
and bring an end to history.

You were there while I was being formed in utter seclusion! You saw me before I was born and scheduled each day of my life before I began to breathe. Every day was recorded in your book! (Psalm 139:15-16, TLB)

And then shall many be offended, and shall betray one another, and shall hate one another. (Matthew 24:10)

And when ye shall hear of wars and rumors of wars, be ye not troubled: for *such thing* must needs be; but the end *shall not be* yet. (Mark 13:7)

Our Father which art in heaven, Hallowed be thy name. Thy kingdom come, Thy will be done in earth, as it is in heaven. (Matthew 6: 9b-13)

And this gospel of the kingdom shall be preached in all the world for a witness unto all nations; and then shall the end come. (Matthew 24:14)

And he hath on his vesture and on his thigh a name written, King Of Kings, And Lord Of Lords. (Revelation 19:16)

Chapter 4

God: The Three in One

The morning breeze that we can feel,
we cannot see, although it's real.
Dew condenses to form the clouds;
the globe they then will soon enshroud.

But when we reach into the sky
to catch a cloud that passes by,
it wisps away too quick to grasp,
no "substance" there for us to clasp.

That same air that we can't see
is wind that makes the clouds to flee.
And air and wind are everywhere,
throughout the planet's atmosphere.

When the clouds become a storm,
rain or hail or snow is formed.
No longer can the sky contain
the heavy weight the dew has gained.

Many attempts have been made to explain the Trinity known as God: the Three in One, Father, Son, and Holy Spirit.

This poem is another such attempt.

The present description may or may not resonate with readers. To the extent it does resonate, it could help clarify a reality that has been an incomprehensible mystery for most people throughout the world, including Christians.

There is agreement between the poetry and the Scriptures in that both use wind in their analogies.

> The wind bloweth where it listeth, and thou hearest the sound thereof, but canst not tell whence it cometh, and whither it goeth: so is every one that is born of the Spirit. (John 3:8)

> Lightning and hail, snow and clouds, stormy winds that do his bidding. (Psalm 148:8, NIV)

> He says to the snow, 'Fall on the earth...',
> (Job 37:6a, NIV)

When snow has settled on the ground,
each flake is to another bound.
Unlike the clouds that fly away,
each flake claims a place to stay.

Then children playing in the snow
find a way to make it grow
to form the image of a man
with head and face and chest and hands.

The snow is "substance" children mold
to make the man they then behold.
Then they romp and laugh and cheer—
they made a man from atmosphere.

The features of this imagery
help solve a major mystery—
God, the Father, Christ the Son,
the Holy Spirit, the Three in One.

Throughout the Scriptures, snow refers to purity, in one sense, or being essential to life and growth in another sense.

> Come now, let us reason together, says the Lord: though your sins are like scarlet, they shall be as white as snow; though they are red like crimson, they shall become like wool. (Isaiah 1:18)

> He spreads the snow like wool and scatters the frost like ashes. (Psalm 147:16, NIV)

> His appearance was like lightning, and his clothes were white as snow. (Matthew 28:3, NIV)

> As I looked, thrones were set in place, and the Ancient of Days took his seat. His clothing was as white as snow; the hair of his head was white like wool. (Daniel 7:8, NIV)

> The hair on his head was white like wool, as white as snow, and his eyes were like blazing fire. (Revelation 1:14, NIV)

> As the rain and snow come down from heaven and stay upon the ground to water the earth, and cause the grain to grow and to produce seed for the farmer and bread for the hungry, so also is my word. I send it out, and it al-ways produces fruit. It shall accomplish all I want it to and prosper everywhere I send it. (Isaiah 55:10-11, TLB).

Atmosphere is constant essence;
condensing dew proves its presence.
The dew is something we can see,
the "visual essence" of reality.

God, the Father, like the air,
is always present everywhere.
And the Holy Spirit, whom we can't see,
has power like wind to nth degree.

To complete the three as Deity,
· Christ must be Divinity.
Thus, "Jesus is" the "visual essence"
of the Father/Spirit's power and presence.

The Father, equal with the Son;
the Son and Spirit also One—
God is Holy Trinity,
condensed in Christ's reality.

The poetic imagery lets us picture Jesus as the visible expression of the eternal, ever-present, all-knowing God. Jesus is the innocent, sinless Son of Man, who visibly represented God while He was on earth. Now, the Holy Spirit, who also possesses unlimited power, is God's earthly representative.

> I can *never* be lost to your Spirit! I can *never* get away from my God! If I go up to heaven, you are there; if I go down to the place of the dead, you are there. If I ride the morning winds to the farthest oceans, even there your hand will guide me, your strength will support me. (Psalm 139:7-10, TLB)

> And suddenly there came from heaven a sound like a mighty rushing wind, and it filled the entire house where they were sitting. (Acts 2:2)

> Jesus said: "I and the Father are one". (John 10:30)

> Jesus said: "He who has seen Me has seen the Father". (John 14:9)

> All things are delivered unto me of my Father: and no man knoweth the Son, but the Father; neither knoweth any man the Father, save the Son, and he to whomsoever the Son will reveal him. (Matthew 11:27)

> For there are three that bear record in heaven, the Father, the Word [Jesus], and the Holy Ghost: and these three are one. (1 John 5:7)

Chapter 5

God the Father is the Potter

At the time when time began,
and God created man,
the image He designed
was "perfect" in His mind.

The reason for that perfection—
man was God's reflection.
So what He saw in us
was the image of Himself.

What God had first intended,
Adam's sin suspended,
causing God to set up laws
that exposed our human flaws.

Like the man that children mold,
from the snow they then behold,
their attempt at reproduction
is filled with imperfection.

While God's original plan was interrupted by Adam's sin, His will ultimately prevails. Believers who have been forgiven and know His Son Jesus have the glorious hope of an eternity that lives out what God had in mind from the beginning.

> And God said, Let us make man in our image, after our likeness.... So God created man in his own image, in the image of God created he him; male and female created he them. (Genesis 1:26-27)

> And God saw everything that he had made, and, behold, it was very good. (Genesis 1:31)

> By one man's [Adam's] disobedience many were made sinners. (Romans 5:19)

> For all have sinned, and come short of the glory of God. (Romans 6:23)

> The Ten Commandments were given so that all could see the extent of their failure to obey God's laws. (Romans 5:20a, TLB)

> As the Scriptures say, "No one is good—no one in all the world is innocent. No one has ever really followed God's paths or even truly wanted to. Everyone has turned away; all have gone wrong. No one anywhere has kept on doing what is right; not one". (Romans 3:10-12, TLB)

That's why God, the Father,
saw the need to be the Potter.
He molds us, His human clay,
to fashion children that obey.

He is working still
to help us do His will,
so when the molding's done,
we'll be like His "perfect" Son.

The world is our temporary home where God has provided a proving ground for humanity. It's a place where we have the opportunity to be reconciled with God, through *faith* in His Son, Jesus. Those who pass the test will be transformed, even with new bodies when they are resurrected.

> And yet, O Lord, you are our Father. We are the clay and you are the Potter. We are all formed by your hand. (Isaiah 64:8, TLB)

> For it is God which worketh in you both to will and to do of his good pleasure. (Philippians 2:13)

> It will all happen in a moment, in the twinkling of an eye, when the last trumpet is blown. For there will be a trumpet blast from the sky, and all the Christians who have died will suddenly become alive, with new bodies that will never, never die; and then we who are still alive shall suddenly have new bodies too. For our earthly bodies, the ones we have now that can die, must be transformed into heavenly bodies that cannot perish but will live forever. (1 Corinthians 15:52-53, TLB)

> For from the very beginning God decided that those who came to him—and all along he knew who would—should become like his Son, so that his Son would be the first, with many brothers. (Romans 8:29, TLB)

Chapter 6

The Master's Perfect Plan

When evil deeds caused man to fall,
and sin emerged to damn us all,
God found a way for fallen man
to be redeemed and saved again.

It's in the heart where wrongs reside
and damning deeds and sin abide.
That's where sin-seeds germinate,
producing fruit of Satan's hate.

But the Master's Plan reveals the Light
that opens eyes to give us sight,
so we can see the path to take,
and God, a new creation make.

Through His Plan and love and grace,
He offers all of every race
the chance to choose His path of Light
that changes hearts from wrong to right.

The Bible tells us how we were originally separated from God and how He now provides a *perfect plan* for us to be restored back to that original relationship.

> Wherefore, as by one man [Adam] sin entered into the world, and death by sin; and so death passed upon all men, for that all have sinned. (Romans 5:12)

> The thief [Satan] cometh not, but for to steal, and to kill, and to destroy. (John 10:10)

> The heart is deceitful above all things and desperately wicked. (Jeremiah 17:9)

> Be not deceived; God is not mocked: for whatsoever a man soweth, that shall he also reap. For he that soweth to his flesh shall of the flesh reap corruption. (Galatians 6:7-8a)

> Neither is there salvation in any other: for there is none other name under heaven given among men, whereby we must be saved. (Acts 4:12)

> Jesus said: "I am the Light of the world. So if you follow me, you won't be stumbling through the darkness, for living light will flood your path". (John 8:12, TLB)

> Therefore if any man be in Christ, he is a new creature (creation): old things are passed away; behold, all things are become new. (2 Corinthians 5:17)

> For the grace of God that bringeth salvation hath appeared to all men, teaching us that, denying ungodliness and worldly lusts, we should live soberly, righteously, and godly, in this present world. (Titus 2:11-12a)

It's in he head where thoughts aspire.
It's in the heart where will desires.
It's in the hands where deeds transpire,
and all are good that God inspires.

For in the Master's Perfect Plan,
He inspires His thoughts in man,
so we achieve His purposes,
and He fulfills His promises.

The story here in poetry
contains both promises and prophecies,
where promises are proved by faith,
and prophecies on facts are based.

Faith and fact both lead to truth
that even science agrees is proof—
God exists and keeps His Word,
which demands response when it is heard.

God's order of *inspiration* is from the head to the heart to the hands.

> Whatsoever things are true, whatsoever things are honest, whatsoever things are just, whatsoever things are pure, whatsoever things are lovely, whatsoever things are of good report; if there be any virtue, and if there be any praise, *think* on these things. (Philippians 4:8)

> For it is God which worketh in you both *to will* and *to do* of his good pleasure. (Philippians 2:13, emphasis mine)

> Now faith is the substance of things hoped for, the evidence of things not seen. (Hebrews 11:1)

> For the prophecy came not in old time by the will of man: but holy men of God spake as they were moved by the Holy Ghost. (1 Peter 1:21)

> But you, Daniel, shut up the words, and seal the book until the time of the end; many shall run to and fro, and knowledge shall increase. (Daniel 12:4)

> When he, the Spirit of truth [the Holy Spirit] is come, he will guide you into all truth. (John 16:13)

> Sanctify them by Your truth. Your word is truth. (John 17:17)

> But be ye doers of the word, and not hearers only, deceiving your own selves. (James 1:22)

No greater choice on earth is made
than one for which the course is laid
to let our conscience be our guide
to holy Truth that God provides.

His Holy Spirit points to the Way,
on which by faith we need to stay,
until God's Son, as prophesied,
comes in the clouds to get His Bride.

In the Master's great design,
He even uses thoughts of mine,
to help others know and learn,
how near it is to Christ's return.

But the message in this poetry
is more than "proving" prophecy.
It's meant to change your destiny,
from death to life, eternally.

The topic at hand could not be more significant. It must be addressed at some point by everyone with the capacity for behavioral accountability.

> For God so loved the world that he gave his only begotten son that whosoever believeth in him should not perish but have everlasting life. (John 3:16)

> For whosoever will save his life shall lose it; but whosoever shall lose his life for my sake and the gospel's, the same shall save it. For what shall it profit a man, if he shall gain the whole world, and lose his own soul? (Mark 8:35-36)

> I have set before you life and death, blessing and cursing: therefore choose life that both thou and thy seed may live: That thou mayest love the Lord thy God, and that thou mayest obey his voice, and that thou mayest cleave unto him: for he is thy life... (Deuteronomy 30:19-20a)

> But the Comforter, which is the Holy Ghost, whom the Father will send in my name, he shall teach you all things, and bring all things to your remembrance, whatsoever I have said unto you. (John 14:26)

> For the wages of sin is death; but the gift of God is eternal life through Jesus Christ our Lord. (Romans 6:23)

If there's a void deep in your soul
that God must fill to make you whole,
then "listen" to His still small voice;
He's calling you to make a choice!

For those who hear, or see, or read
have gained new knowledge they must heed,
and many prophecies are yet reserved
of facts and proofs to be observed.

And every Truth that is a proof
is another voice of God's reproof,
and every knock on your heart's door,
you must not choose to just ignore.

While Adam's fall brought death to all,
the Master's Plan is mercy's call
to purge your heart of every sin
so God can come and dwell within.

I will send you the Comforter—the Holy Spirit, the source of all truth. He will come to you from the Father and will tell you all about me. And you also must tell everyone about me because you have been with me from the beginning. (John 15:26-27)

And thine ears shall hear a word behind thee, saying, this is the way, walk ye in it, when ye turn to the right hand, and when ye turn to the left. (Isaiah 30:21)

For his Holy Spirit speaks to us deep in our hearts and tells us that we really are God's children. And since we are his children, we will share his treasures—for all God gives to his Son Jesus is now ours too. But if we are to share his glory, we must also share his suffering. (Romans 6:16-17, TLB)

Be ye doers of the word, and not hearers only, deceiving your own selves. (James 1:22)

Behold, I stand at the door, and knock: if any man hear my voice, and open the door, I will come in to him, and will sup with him, and he with me. (Revelation 3:20)

The sin of this one man, Adam, caused *death to be king over all,* but all who will take God's gift of forgiveness and acquittal are *kings of life* because of this one man, Jesus Christ. Yes, Adam's *sin* brought *punishment* to all, but Christ's *righteousness* makes men *right with God,* so that they can live. Adam caused many to be sinners because he *disobeyed* God, and Christ caused many to be made acceptable to God because he *obeyed.* (Romans 5:17-19, emphasis mine)

And we all can be saved in this same way, by coming to Christ, no matter who we are or what we have been like. Yes, all have sinned; all fall short of God's glorious ideal; yet now God declares us "not guilty" of offending him if we trust in Jesus Christ, who in his kindness freely takes away our sins. (Romans 3:22b-24, TLB)

In the Master's Perfect Plan
is Jesus Christ, the Son of Man,
who is to us a pure example
of God Himself indwelling people.

God has called us all to come
to give our hearts to His dear Son,
so He can make our heart's desire
to do His will through His great power.

All who choose the path that's right
will find it leads to Truth and Light,
and Jesus Christ, whom we obey,
guides and helps us in the Way.

Now you know what you must do
to put God's Plan to work for you,
so Love and Truth that's in your heart
help light the path that others start.

Jesus is the model we are asked to emulate; the Holy Spirit gives *believers* the *power* to do that:

> My grace is sufficient for thee: for my strength is made perfect in weakness. Most gladly therefore will I rather glory in my infirmities, that the power of Christ may rest upon me. (2 Corinthians 12:9)

> He that believeth on him is not condemned: but he that believeth not is condemned already, because he hath not believed in the name of the only begotten Son of God. (John 3:18)

> Delight thyself also in the Lord: and he shall give thee the desires of thine heart. Commit thy way unto the Lord; trust also in him; and he shall bring it to pass. And he shall bring forth thy righteousness as the light, and thy judgment as the noonday. Rest in the Lord, and wait patiently for him. (Psalm 37:4-7a)

> I pray that your hearts will be flooded with light so that you can see something of the future he has called you to share. (Ephesians 1:18a, 19, TLB)

> Let your light so shine before men, that they may see your good works, and glorify your Father which is in heaven. (Matthew 5:16)

> For I am not ashamed of this Good News about Christ. It is God's powerful method of bringing all who believe it to heaven. (Romans 1:16a)

Chapter 7

Jesus' Birth

How did prophets come to know
so many thousand years ago
that a virgin would give birth
to the Son of God on earth?

They even said of Him:
He'd be born in Bethlehem.
In a stable, in a barn,
in a manger, a King was born.

A star from distant space
shined on that Holy place,
guiding wise men as they came,
bringing gifts to worship Him.

Immanuel: God had come.
Jesus, Messiah, Anointed One,
pure, perfect, innocent,
Savior, Shepherd, Providence.

Jesus is the central figure in God's plan to reconcile man back to Himself, back to the *being* He created in His own image. Through Jesus' miraculous birth, His sinless life, His final sacrifice on the Cross, the price was paid with His blood, and the way was paved for our salvation.

> Therefore the Lord himself shall give you a sign; Behold, a virgin shall conceive, and bear a son. (Isaiah 7:14)

> But thou, Bethlehem Ephratah, though thou be littlea-mong the thousands of Judah, yet out of there shall he come forth unto me that is to be ruler in Israel; whose oings forth have been from of old; from everlasting. (Micah 5:2)

> Ye shall find the babe wrapped in swaddling clothes lying in a manger. (Matthew 2:5-7)

> They shall call his name Immanuel, which being interpreted is, God with us. (Matthew 1:23)

> Lo, the star, which they saw in the east, went before them, till it came and stood over where the young child was...and (they) fell down, and worshipped him...they presented unto him gifts. (Matthew 2:9-11)

An angel formed a Heavenly choir,
recording songs that marked the hour.
Expressions of its gleeful joy
were all about that baby boy.

Mary knew within her heart—
an angel told her at the start—
the boy that she would bear,
with the world she'd have to share.

Those secrets that she knew
did, in fact, come true.
Now history has confirmed,
what prophets had discerned.

Jesus, the Messiah then,
would live and die and rise again.
2,000 years have passed since then;
He promised us, He'll come again.

There are over three hundred prophecies in the Old Testament which predicted the coming Messiah and His earthly life and death. Jesus Christ fulfilled every one of those prophecies, without exception. The statistical probability of their occurrence by an imposter, anyone other than the authentic Messiah, God incarnate, is too great to calculate.

> And suddenly there was with the angel a multitude of the heavenly host praising God, and saying, glory to God in the highest, and on earth peace, good will toward men. (Luke 2:13-14)

> The angel replied, "The Holy Spirit shall come upon you, and the power of God shall overshadow you; so the baby born to you will be utterly holy—the Son of God". (Luke 1:35, TLB)

> I go to prepare a place for you. And... I will come again, and receive you unto myself; that where I am, there ye may be also. (John 14:2-3)

The signs of His return
are for us to now discern.
He sent them at creation
to ensure our preparation.

But the reason for His birth,
and the life He lived on earth,
was to show us how to live,
so to Him our hearts we'd give.

For all who then are born again,
eternal life He gives to them.
In Him we have great joy and peace.
In fact, He is the Prince of Peace.

He also is the Living Light
that helps us find each path that's right.
His Word is wisdom we must know,
so through us, His Light will glow.

As the day approaches for Christ's Second Coming, Jerusalem will be surrounded by enemies, as we see occurring in the news every day in recent years. Especially at that time, all of the followers of Christ are instructed to "look up!" Why? We believe that instruction was given because God planned from the beginning to send messages to His children through the sun, moon and stars, signaling the nearness of Christ's return. We devote much of a chapter to God's signals in the sky.

> And God said, "Let there be lights in the firmament of the heaven to divide the day from the night; and let them be for signs, and for seasons, and for days, and years". (Genesis 1:14)

> Jerusalem shall be trodden down of the Gentiles, until the times of the Gentiles be fulfilled. And there shall be signs in the sun, and in the moon, and in the stars. (Luke 21:24)

> ...for the powers of heaven shall be shaken. ...look up, and lift up your heads; for your redemption draweth nigh. (Luke 21:26b-28)

> Verily, verily, I say unto you, He that believeth on me, the works that I do shall he do also; and greater *works* than these shall he do; because I go unto my Father. (John 14:12)

> For a child will be born to us, a son will be given to us; And the government will rest on His shoulders; And His name will be called Wonderful Counselor, Mighty God Eternal Father, Prince of Peace. (Isaiah 9:6)

> Jesus said to the people, "I am the Light of the world. So if you follow me, you won't be stumbling through the darkness, for living light will flood your path". (John 8:12, TLB)

> Let your light so shine before men, that they may see your good works, and glorify your Father which is in heaven. (Matthew 5:16)

He came down from Heaven above
to bring to all His Truth and Love.
"So many" blessings came to earth
that Holy night of Jesus' birth.

For he hath made him to be sin for us, who knew no sin; that we might be made the righteousness of God in him. (2 Corinthians 5:21)

But as many as received him, to them gave he power to become the sons of God, even to them that believe on his name: (John 1:12)

What can we ever say to such wonderful things as these? If God is on our side, who can ever be against us? Since he did not spare even his own Son for us but gave him up for us all, won't he also surely give us everything else? (Romans 8:31-32)

Who dares accuse us whom God has chosen for his own? Will God? No! He is the one who has forgiven us and given us right standing with himself. (Romans 8:33)

Who then will condemn us? Will Christ? *No!* For he is the one who died for us and came back to life again for us and is sitting at the place of highest honor next to God, pleading for us there in heaven. (Romans 8:34)

Chapter 8

Jesus' Mission

God designed a holy plan
to redeem the souls of sinful man.
On the Cross, Christ gave His life.
That's what it took to pay the price.

Christ's mission here on planet Earth
was focused on our spirit's birth.
He came to conquer death and doom
and did that when He left the Tomb.

He rose to be "Thy Kingdom Come";
His mission here was almost done.
He left our sins back in the grave.
To life eternal, the Way was paved.

His grace extends for us to claim;
He answers prayer, prayed in His Name.
He came to save us from our sins
and give us perfect hearts again.

The cited Scriptures are the words of the living God that inspired the poetry. They begin the story of Jesus' mission here on Earth, the greatest story ever told.

> But God...even when we were dead in trespasses, made us alive together with Christ. (Ephesians 2:4-6)

> For even the Son of Man did not come to be served, but to serve, and to give his life as a ransom for many. (Mark 10:45)

> Unless one is born of water and the Spirit, he cannot enter the kingdom of God. (John 3:5-7)

> Do not be afraid, for I know that you seek Jesus who was crucified. He is not here: for *He is risen,* as He said. (Matthew 28:5-6)

> After this manner therefore pray ye: Our Father which art in heaven, Hallowed be thy name. *Thy kingdom come,* Thy will be done in earth, as it is in heaven. (Matthew 6:9-10)

> He will subdue our iniquities; and thou wilt cast all their sins into the depths of the sea. (Micah 7:19)

> Whatever you ask in My name, that will I do, so that the Father may be glorified in the Son. (John 14:13)

> Be ye therefore perfect, even as your Father which is in heaven is perfect. (Matthew 5:48)

He came to show us how to live
and how to Him our lives to give.
He came to tell us: "Follow me",
so His disciples we would be.

We began as natural creatures;
now we're partakers of His nature.
On our behalf His Spirit pleads;
He came to meet our every need.

He came to seek our fellowship
and nurture our relationship.
He came to be our closest friend,
loving, caring without end.

His Word when heard brings truth and peace,
a fact that helps our faith increase.
He came to bless all who believe,
in that Truth that they receive.

The story continues, filled with instruction, hope, and promise:

Whosoever will come after me, let him deny himself, and take up his cross, and follow me. (Mark 8:34)

Follow me, and I will make you fishers of men. (Matthew 4:19)

Whereby are given unto us exceeding great and precious promises: that by these ye might be partakers of thedivine nature, having escaped the corruption that is in the world through lust. (2 Peter 1:4)

But my God shall supply all your need according to his riches in glory by Christ Jesus. (Philippians 4:19).

If we walk in the light, as he is in the light, we have fellowship one with another, and the blood of JesusChrist his Son cleanses us from all sin. (1 John 1:7)

Now you are my friends, since I have told you everything the Father told me. (John 15:15)

Faith comes by hearing and hearing by the Word of God. (Romans 10:17)

Blessed is the man...whose delight is in the law of the Lord and in His law doeth he meditate day and night. (Psalms 1:1-3)

He came to be the Living Light
that keeps us on the path that's right.
He came to help us overcome,
when all our human strength is gone.

How many times have threats and fears
been turned away by angels near,
or major problems, too extreme,
then through prayer, He intervened?

He came to shield our very soul,
blessing us with self-control.
Goodness, kindness and forbearance,
also fruit born from endurance.

Faith and Hope and Love,
like showers from above,
fall on us in Holy power,
sufficient strength for every hour.

God's plan for our redemption is the perfect expression of His love, grace, and mercy fulfilled in the birth, life, death, and resurrection of His Son, Jesus.

> I am the light of the world, if you keep on following me, you won't be stumbling through the darkness, for living light will flood your path. (John 8:12, TLB)

> And they overcame him by the blood of the Lamb, and by the word of their testimony. (Revelation 12:11)

> For he will command his angels concerning you to guard you in all your ways. (Psalms 91:11)

> In the day of my trouble I call upon you, for you answer me. (Psalms 86:7)

> But the fruit of the Spirit is love, joy, peace, forbearance, kindness, goodness, faithfulness, gentleness and self-control. (Galatians 5:22-23)

> And now these three remain: faith, hope and love but the greatest of these is love. (1 Corinthians 13:13)

> I can do all things through Christ who strengthens me. (Philippians 4:13)

These blessings, just the start,
for all who have a perfect heart.
He came to do even more,
we are asked to trust Him for.

He came to give us life eternal,
when we have closed our earthly journal.
Now we seek to tell His story,
so all who hear it give Him glory.

A right relationship with God has many benefits, as these verses record.

> The eyes of the Lord search back and forth across the whole earth looking for people whose hearts are perfect toward Him so He can show His great power in helping them. (2 Chronicles 16:9, TLB)

> Delight thyself also in the Lord: and he shall give thee the desires of thine heart. Commit thy way unto the Lord; trust also in him; and he shall bring it to pass. (Psalms 37:4-5)

> I write these things to you who believe in the name of the Son of God so that you may know that you have eternal life. (2 John 5:13)

> Be ready always to give an answer to every man that asketh you a reason of the hope that is in you.... (2 Peter 3:15)

> O God, in mercy bless us; let your face beam with joy as you look down at us. Send us around the world with the news of our saving power and your eternal plan for all mankind. (Psalms 67:1-2, TLB)

> But ye shall receive power, after that the Holy Ghost is come upon you: and ye shall be witnesses unto me both in Jerusalem, and in all Judea, and in Samaria, and unto the uttermost part of the earth. (Acts 1:8)

Chapter 9

Jesus' Sacrifice

Jesus Christ came down from Heaven,
the Son of God, a Holy human —
innocent from earliest days;
sinless in all His ways.

He came to do His Father's will
and wants us to the same fulfill.
He came to earth to set in motion
the plan that leads us to salvation.

He came to die upon the Cross,
knowing well how great the cost.
The lashes cut, the skin was peeled;
by those stripes, we are healed.

The nails that bound Him to the tree
changed the course of history.
The pain from thorns that He endured —
its hate expressed, our hope assured.

From His birth to His ascension, Jesus was completely innocent of any wrong doing, and that is the ultimate outcome for all who have a personal relationship with Christ. They too are innocent because they are covered by Christ's blood. What a marvelous opportunity; what a glorious hope, for all who believe.

He came from the Father and entered the world. (John 16:28)

God made him who had no sin to be sin for us... (2 Corinthians 5:21)

Jesus asked: "Did you not know, I must be about my Father's business?" (Luke 2:49)

He said: "I am come that you might have life, and that you might have it more abundantly". (John 10:10)

He also said: "I lay it [my life] down of myself. I have power to lay it down, and I have power to take it again". (John 10:18)

But he was wounded for our transgressions, he was bruised for our iniquities: the chastisement of our peace was upon him; and with his stripes we are healed. (Isaiah 53:5).

You, with the help of wicked men, put him to death by nailing him to the cross. (Acts 2:23)

[They] then twisted together a crown of thorns and set it on his head. Then they knelt in front of him and mocked him. (Matthew 27:29)

The drops of blood that stained his face—
eternal emblems of His grace.
The blood that sent Him to the grave—
His love poured out, our souls to save.

His death became the sacrifice
that frees us from an equal price.
They thrust a spear into His side
even after he had died.

The wound gushed forth a crimson flow
cleansing sinners pure as snow.
No greater love could Christ apply
than for the world He came to die.

The wine we drink at sacrament
reminds of Christ's atonement.
His Word is now our Bread of life,
as we recall His sacrifice.

Christ's death was excruciating, both physically and emotionally. His body suffered from the painful cruelties; His heart was broken from the mockery of our sins. He also died alone. Even His Father turned away, but Christ's willing sacrifice was a sufficient price for our atonement. It is the payment for the promised gift of eternal life for all who repent and believe.

> God presented Christ as a sacrifice of atonement, through the shedding of his blood... (Romans 3:25)

> ...that we, having died to sins, might live for righteous-ness. (1 Peter 2:24)

> He was already dead...one of the soldiers pierced His side with a spear, and immediately blood and water came out. (John 19:33-34)

> The blood of Jesus Christ His Son cleanses us from all sin. (1 John 1:7)

> Greater love hath no man than this that a man lay down his life for his friends. Ye are my friends, if ye do whatsoever I command you. (John 15:13-14)

> And he took the cup, and gave thanks, and gave it to them, saying, "Drink ye all of it, for this is my blood of the new testament, which is shed for many for the remission of sins". (Matthew 26:27-28)

> I am the bread of life. If anyone eats of this bread, he will live forever; and the bread that I shall give is my flesh, which I shall give for the life of the world. (John 6:48, 51b)

Chapter 10

I Am the Light of the World

On the path in darkest night,
without a ray or beam of light,
with many hazards lurking near;
there is much for us to fear.

That's how it is with man,
where there's unforgiven sin.
When Satan is the guide,
death and danger lurk beside.

God has put in our control,
His Way to save our very soul,
when our life we give to Him,
and Jesus comes to dwell within.

Jesus then is Living Light,
who guides us on a path that's bright.
No longer need we walk in fear;
by "The Light of the World", the Way is clear.

Jesus said: "I am the Light of the World..." (John 8:12)

The world lives in spiritual darkness; it doesn't have a clue about what it means to walk in the light of the Word, the Light intended for the entire world.

What an honor and privilege it is to know and walk and live in fellowship with Jesus, the unquenchable, eternal, Living Light; and the Light is not exclusive.

"Whosoever will may come". (Revelation 22:17)

Be sober, be vigilant; because your adversary the devil, as a roaring lion, walketh about, seeking whom he may devour. (1 Peter 5:8)

The light of the body is the eye: if therefore thine eye be single, thy whole body shall be full of light. But if thine eye be evil, thy whole body shall be full of darkness. If therefore the light that is in thee be darkness, how great is that darkness! (Matthew 6:22-23)

Jesus said to the people, "I am the Light of the world. So if you follow me, you won't be stumbling through the darkness, for living light will flood your path." (John 8:12)

Chapter 11

I Am the Way, the Truth and the Life

How can we be sure to know
the best of paths down which to go,
or where to look for Truth
when faith's our basic proof?

It's common in our day,
for people now to say:
"There're many paths to God,
which we can choose to trod".

When Jesus walked the paths of earth,
He said: We need a second birth.
He alone forgives our sin;
it's through Him, we're born again.

His Word is clear; we hear His voice;
there is no other valid choice!
"I am the Way the Truth the Life".
The path to God?—through Jesus Christ.

"I am the Way the Truth and the Life" (John 14:6).

What strong words, and they are exclusive in the sense that no one or no thing can substitute for Him.

Jesus affirms that exclusiveness by continuing, in effect: there is no other way to the Father, to Heaven, or to eternal life. There are no other options; no reason to be confused; no excuse for questioning the choice; Jesus leaves no doubt. The message is straightforward, positive, assuring, and firm.

> And thine ears shall hear a word behind thee, saying: "This is the way, walk ye in it, when ye turn to the right hand, and when ye turn to the left". (Isaiah 30:21)

> Jesus answered, "Verily, verily, I say unto thee, Except a man be born of water and of the Spirit, he cannot enter into the kingdom of God. That which is born of the flesh is flesh; and that which is born of the Spirit is spirit. Marvel not that said unto thee, Ye must be born again". (John 3:5-7)

> Jesus saith unto him, "I am the way, the truth, and the life: no man cometh unto the Father, but by me". (John 14:6)

Chapter 12

I Am the Door

Each decision that we make
puts us on a path to take,
and every path that we explore,
takes us to another door.

Unless Christ is there to guide,
doors of evil open wide.
Satan tempts us to come in;
his doors to pleasure lead to sin.

He lies to cleverly deceive,
causing many to disbelieve.
He robs them of God's best,
which finally ends in death.

Jesus wants to be our guide:
"I am the door", come on inside.
He beckons us to live for Him;
eternal life is found in Him.

All of the "I Am's," including "I am the door," paint pictures of common images in our mind that simplify Jesus' awesome majesty, thereby endearing Himself to us and making it easy to identify with Him.

Also, all of the "I Ams" draw us toward a personal relationship with Jesus, through whom we have access to the Father, to Heaven, and to eternal life.

> Then said Jesus unto them again: "Verily, verily, I say unto you, I am the door of the sheep. All that ever came before me are thieves and robbers: but the sheep did not hear them. I am the door: by me if any man enter in, he shall be saved, and shall go in and out, and find pasture". (John 10:7-9)

> For through him we both have access by one Spirit unto the Father. (Ephesians 2:18)

Chapter 13

I Am the Good Shepherd

The sheep meander on the hill;
they nibble grass to get their fill.
At times they pause to quench their thirst
and little lambs of mothers nurse.

The shepherd's there to tend his flock,
to keep it safe when danger knocks.
But in the course of every day,
a lamb will often stray away.

When we with sheep our lives compare,
our Good Shepherd, we know is there,
making sure our needs are met,
protecting us from evil threats.

Our Shepherd knew that we would stray.
He even knew the price to pay
to redeem us when we're lost.
He gave His life to pay that cost.

The image of a shepherd conveys gentleness and tender, loving patience. A shepherd is also alert and sensitive to danger and is a protector from attacks from any source. A shepherd seeks to find one that goes astray. How better to describe Jesus, our Good Shepherd, who possesses all of these gracious attributes?

> He shall feed his flock like a shepherd: he shall gather he lambs with his arm, and carry them in his bosom, and shall gently lead those that are with young. (Isaiah 40:11)

> How think ye? If a man have an hundred sheep, and one of them be gone astray, doth he not leave the ninety and nine, and goeth into the mountains, and seeketh that which is gone astray? (Matthew 18:12)

> The Lord is my shepherd; I shall not want. He maketh me to lie down in green pastures: he leadeth me beside the still waters. He restoreth my soul: he leadeth me in the paths of righteousness for his name's sake. (Psalms 23:1-3)

> I am the good shepherd, and know my sheep, and am known of mine. As the Father knoweth me, even so know I the Father: and I lay down my life for the sheep. And other sheep I have, which are not of this fold: them also I must bring, and they shall hear my voice; and there shall be one fold, and one shepherd. (John 10:14-16)

> I am the good shepherd: the good shepherd giveth his life for the sheep. (John 10:11)

Chapter 14

I Am the Bread of Life

Jesus is the Son of Man—
first a babe, a boy, and then a man.
He was tempted, without sin;
He knows we're weak and not like Him.

He walked and talked and lived with us;
He cared and loved and died for us.
His Word is Truth, He bestowed;
His life, a model, we behold.

He finished what He came to do,
to make a Way for me and you.
Our sins are covered by His blood;
His Word, like bread, our spirit's food.

"I am the Bread of Life", Christ said.
It's by His Word that you are fed.
It will to you its strength impart,
when it is hidden in your heart.

Throughout history, bread has been a staple in the daily diet of human beings. God even sent manna, like bread, down from heaven, on which the children of Israel survived for forty years in the desert. However, bread also is a symbol of the Word of God, on which Christians must feed for their spiritual lives to thrive.

> I am the Bread of Life! When your fathers in the wilderness ate bread from the skies, they all died. But the Bread from heaven gives eternal life to everyone who eats it. I am that Living Bread that came down out of heaven. Anyone eating this Bread shall live forever; this Bread is my flesh given to redeem humanity. (John 6:48-51)

> Our fathers did eat manna in the desert; as it is written, He gave them bread from heaven to eat. Then Jesus said unto them: "Verily, verily, I say unto you, Moses gave you not that bread from heaven; but my Father giveth you the true bread from heaven. For the bread of God is he which cometh down from heaven, and giveth life unto the world". Then said they unto him, "Lord, evermore give us this bread". And Jesus said unto them, "I am the bread of life: he that cometh to me shall never hunger; and he that believeth on me shall never thirst". (John 6:31-35).

> Man shall not live by bread alone, but by every word that proceedeth out of the mouth of God. (Matthew 4:4)

Chapter 15

I Am the Vine

What did Jesus have in mind
when He claimed: "I am the Vine"?
It is a good analogy,
a lesson in theology.

God, who gardens, prunes at times,
cutting branches from the vines.
The pruning helps our fitness
to be a better witness.

Thus in love and wisdom,
He prepares us for His Kingdom,
and the Holy Spirit empowers,
when His voice we add to ours.

Like a branch that's grafted in,
we in faith abide in Him.
And our fruit at harvest time? —
multiplied through Jesus' Vine.

This poem and these supporting Scriptures invite Christians to participate in the eternal, life-changing, redemptive process of other human beings. There is no higher calling.

> Be ready always to give an answer to every man that asketh you a reason of the hope that is in you with meekness and fear. (1 Peter 3:15)

> I am the true Vine, and my Father is the Gardener. He lops off every branch that doesn't produce. And he prunes those branches that bear fruit for even larger crops. He has already tended you by pruning you back for greater strength and usefulness by means of the commands I gave you. Take care to live in me, and letme live in you. For a branch can't produce fruit when severed from the vine. Nor can you be fruitful apart from me. (John 15:1-4, TLB)

> Yes, I am the Vine; you are the branches. Whoever lives in me and I in him shall produce a large crop of fruit. For apart from me you can't do a thing. If anyone separates from me, he is thrown away like a useless branch, withers, and is gathered into a pile with all the others and burned. But if you stay in me and obey my commands, you may ask any request you like, and it will be granted! My true disciples produce bountiful harvests. This brings great glory to my Father. (John 15:5-8, TLB)

> But I will send you the Comforter—the Holy Spirit, the source of all truth. He will come to you from the Father and will tell you all about me. And you also must tell everyone about me because you have been with me from the beginning. (John 15:26-27, TLB)

Chapter 16

I Am the Resurrection and the Life

When we have breathed our last
and life on earth has passed,
our body will take its rest,
then decay back into dust.

What temporal goals we gained;
what possessions we obtained,
will then become as naught,
and over time forgot.

But seeds we planted then
that bore their fruit in Heaven,
the Book of Life records,
for each a just reward.

Jesus died and rose again—
a perfect victor over sin—
through Him we'll have perfection;
life restored at Resurrection.

Then shall the dust return to the earth as it was: and the spirit shall return unto God who gave it. (Ecclesiastes 12:7)

Jesus said unto her, I am the resurrection, and the life: he that believeth in me, though he were dead, yet shall he live. (John 11:25)

While we look not at the things which are seen, but at the things which are not seen: for the things which are seen are temporal; but the things which are not seen are eternal. (2 Corinthians 4:18)

Lay not up for yourselves treasures upon earth, where moth and rust doth corrupt and theives break through and steal. But lay up for yourselves treasures in heaven, where neither moth nor rust doth corrupt, and where thieves do not break through nor steal: For where your treasure is, there will your heart be also. (Matthew 6:19-21)

I saw the dead, great and small, standing before God; and The Books were opened, including the Book of Life. And the dead were judged according to the things written in The Books, each according to the deeds he had done. (Revelation 20:12, TLB)

Death is swallowed up in victory. O death, where is thy sting? O grave, where is thy victory? (1 Corinthians 15:54b-55)

And even we Christians...groan to be released from pain and suffering. We, too, wait anxiously for that day when God will give us our full rights as his children, including the new bodies he has promised us— bodies that will never be sick again and will never die. (Romans 8:23, TLB)

Chapter 17

Jesus' Preparation

Jesus stirred imagination,
when He spoke of preparation.
What is it He is doing
to prepare for our home going?

He gives us glimpses of the future
when we look at heaven's features.
We gaze into the starry sky
and ask ourselves in wonder: "Why"?

If on earth it first began,
at any point from where I am,
an arrow travels into space,
it "never" finds a stopping place.

The planets, stars and new dimensions
are filled with secret information.
God has promised, He will disclose
everything to us He knows.

Jesus said He would go back to Heaven from whence He came, and He would prepare a place for us, so we could live throughout eternity together.

> I go to prepare a place for you. And if I go and prepare a place for you, I will come again, and receive you unto myself; that where I am, there ye may be also. (John 14:2b-3)

> But God hath revealed them unto us by his Spirit: for the Spirit searcheth all things, yea, the deep things of God. Now we have received, not the spirit of the world, but the spirit which is of God; that we might know the things that are freely given to us of God. (1 Corinthians 2:10, 12)

> The heavens declare the glory of God; and the firmament sheweth his handiwork. Day unto day uttereth speech, and night unto night sheweth knowledge. There is no speech nor language, where their voice is not heard. (Psalms 19:1-3)

> Since earliest times men have seen the earth and sky and all God made, and have known of his existence and great eternal power. So they will have no excuse when they stand before God at Judgment Day. (Romans 1:20, TLB)

> For now we see through a glass, darkly; but then face to face: now I know in part; but then shall I know even as also I am known. (1 Corinthians 13:12)

> And I saw a new heaven and a new earth: for the first heaven and the first earth were passed away. (Revelation 21:1)

Tell me how to comprehend
the space beyond where all stars end.
Could it be a place of birth
Of new heavens and new earths?

Those are places of concern,
of which we still must learn.
Eternity's a very long time
for God to do what's on His mind.

When Jesus walked the paths of earth,
He explained the need for a second birth:
'Twas difficult to understand,
a reason to be born again.

The natural birth is physical;
the second birth is spiritual.
The first relates to temporal;
the second, life eternal.

His lord said unto him, Well done, good and faithful servant; thou hast been faithful over a few things, I will make thee ruler over many things: enter thou into the joy of thy lord. (Matthew 25:23)

Nicodemus, a ruler of the Jews,...said unto him, "Rabbi, we know that thou art a teacher come from God: for no man can do these miracles that thou doest, except God be with him". Jesus answered and said unto him, "Verily, verily, I say unto thee: Except a man be born again, he cannot see the kingdom of God". Nicodemus saith unto him, "How can a man be born when he is old? can he enter the second time into his mother's womb, and be born"? (John 3:1-4)

The thief cometh not, but for to steal, and to kill, and to destroy: I am come that they might have life, and that they might have it more abundantly. (John 10:10)

All that the Father gives me will come to me, and whoever comes to me I will never drive away. For I have come down from heaven not to do my will but to do the will of him who sent me. And this is the will of him who sent me, that I shall lose none of all that he has given me, but raise them up at the last day. (John 6:36-39)

Jesus answered, Verily, verily, I say unto thee: Except a man be born of water and of the Spirit, he cannot enter into the kingdom of God. That which is born of the flesh is flesh; and that which is born of the Spirit is spirit. Marvel not that I said unto thee, Ye must be born again. (John 3:5-7)

There are two competing dynasties
seeking human loyalties.
Satan wins when God's rejected,
Jesus finds those He's elected.

Natural man gives full attention
to increasing earth's possessions.
Those possessions can't compare
to all that Jesus has to share.

He even says we can't imagine
how great will be our life in Heaven.
Lots of places to go and see,
many billions of galaxies.

Our new address, we are told,
will be along a street of gold.
Our home is ours, a personal mansion,
2,000 years in its expansion.

Cosmologists at the University of California, Santa Cruz, and the HUDF09 Team recently applied technologies, which allowed them to estimate the number of galaxies in the universe to be between 100 and 200 billion.[14]

> And he said, This will I do: I will pull down my barns, and build greater; and there will I bestow all my fruits and my goods. And I will say to my soul, Soul, thou hast much goods laid up for many years; take thine ease, eat,drink, and be merry. But God said unto him, "Thou fool, this night thy soul shall be required of thee: then whoseshall those things be, which thou hast provided? So is he that layeth up treasure for himself, and is not rich toward God". (Luke 12:18-21)

> For what shall it profit a man, if he shall gain the whole world, and lose his own soul? Mark 8:36.

> Eye hath not seen, nor ear heard, neither have entered into the heart of man, the things which God hath prepared for them that love him. (1 Corinthians 2:9)

> And the street of the city was pure gold. (Revelation 21:21b)

> In my Father's house are many mansions: if it were not so, I would have told you. I go to prepare a place for you. (John 14:2)

> And there shall be no night there; and they need nocandle, neither light of the sun; for the Lord God giveth them light: and they shall reign for ever and ever. (Revelation 22:5)

> And God shall wipe away all tears from their eyes; and there shall be no more death, neither sorrow, nor crying, neither shall there be any more pain: for the former things are passed away. (Revelation 21:4)

No longer will the skies be gray,
our tears will all be wiped away.
Pain and sorrow will be gone,
no fear again of being alone.

Over there, there's no disease,
or causes of emergencies.
Unlike our body of the past,
the new one, built to last.

But greater than all of these
are other types of mysteries.
All will gather 'round the Throne,
millions in one massive throng.

Kneeling in humility,
praising God in unity.
Oh the beauty of the song;
in perfect harmony, 'twill be sung.

While we express our joy in praise and worship out of hearts filled with love and peace here, those expressions will continue in Heaven, spontaneously, forever.

And even we Christians, although we have the Holy Spirit within us as a foretaste of future glory, also groan to be released from pain and suffering. We, too, wait anxiously for that day when God will give us our full rights as his children, including the new bodies he has promised us—bodies that will never be sick again and will never die. (Romans 8:23, TLB)

Lo, a great multitude, which no man could number, of all nations, and kindreds, and people, and tongues, stood before the throne, and before the Lamb, clothed with white robes, and palms in their hands; and cried with a loud voice, saying, Salvation to our God which sitteth upon the throne, and unto the Lamb. And all the angels stood round about the throne, and about the elders and the four beasts, and fell before the throne on their faces, and worshipped God, Saying, "Amen: Blessing, and glory, and wisdom, and thanksgiving, and honor, and power, and might, be unto our God for ever and ever. Amen". (Revelation 7:9)

For there are three that bear record in heaven, the Father, the Word (the Son), and the Holy Ghost: and these three are one. (1 John 5:7)

Another anthem is beginning,
through corridors of Heaven ringing,
building to a Loud crescendo,
reaching every mansion window.

Choral songs with separate parts,
with symphony and heavenly harps.
How sweet the sound for all to hear;
the music here cannot compare.

"King of Kings, Lord of Lords,
we lift our praise in one accord.
We worship you for you are worthy;
we honor you and give you glory".

The acuity of our senses here—
much less than when we're over there—
will contrast in its degree,
like "one" to "a hundred three".

And I heard a sound from heaven like the roaring of a great waterfall or the rolling of mighty thunder. It was the singing of a choir accompanied by harps. (Revelation 14:2)

And he hath on his vesture and on his thigh a name written, King Of Kings, and Lord Of Lords. (Revelation 19:16)

And he carried me away in the spirit to a great and high mountain, and shewed me that great city, the holy Jerusalem, descending out of heaven from God, Having the glory of God: and her light was like unto a stone most precious, even like a jasper stone, clear as crystal. (Revelation 21:10-11)

And the city lieth foursquare, and the length...and the breadth and the height of it are equal. (Revelation 21:16)

And the building of the wall of it was of jasper: and the city was pure gold, like unto clear glass. And the foundations of the wall of the city were garnished with all manner of precious stones. The first foundation was jasper; the second, sapphire; the third, a chalcedony; the fourth, an emerald; The fifth, sardonyx; the sixth, sardius; the seventh, chrysolyte; the eighth, beryl; the ninth, a topaz; the tenth, a chrysoprasus; the eleventh, a jacinth; the twelfth, an amethyst. (Revelation 21:18-20)

And the twelve gates were twelve pearls: every several gate was of one pearl: and the street of the city was pure gold, as it were transparent glass. (Revelation 21:21)

"Worthy is The Great I Am—
the perfect, sacrificial Lamb!
Father, Son, and Spirit, One.
Almighty God! The Three in One".

Something about humanity
limits our capability
and dulls our sensitivity
to feel the full intensity.

The senses we here treasure
that bring us so much pleasure,
in Heaven: exquisite quality,
plus intensity and quantity.

The bottom line is this:
you do not want to miss
Heaven's eternal bliss.
But none get in without a pass!

And the peace of God, which transcends all under-
standing, will guard your hearts and your minds in
Christ Jesus. (Philippians 4:7)

I have loved you even as the Father has loved me.
Live within my love. When you obey me you are
living in my love, just as I obey my Father and live
in his love. I have told you this so that you will be
filled with my joy. Yes, your cup of joy will overflow!
(John 15:9-11)

And God shall wipe away all tears from their eyes;
and there shall be no more death, neither sorrow, nor
crying, neither shall there be any more pain: for the
former things are passed away. (Revelation 21:4-5)

...in the last days perilous times shall come. For men
shall be...lovers of pleasures more than lovers of
God; having a form of godliness, but denying the
power thereof: from such turn away. (2 Timothy 3:
1b, 2a, 4b)

I am the way, the truth, and the life: no man cometh
unto the Father, but by me. (John 14:6)

But the Comforter, which is the Holy Ghost, whom
the Father will send in my name [Jesus], he shall teach
you all things, and bring all things to your remem-
brance, whatsoever I have said unto you. (John 14:26)

The Trinity, an enigmatic mystery,
no equal in all of history,
already has invested
in your "pass," when you are tested.

God pursues us all to come;
receive the gift of His dear Son.
That gift is absolutely free,
not by works of some degree.

The Holy Spirit, God's earthly agent,
gently wooing, loving, patient,
whispering: "This is the Way"!
Attend to "all" He has to say.

Jesus too, seeks out the lost.
His love reached out to pay the cost.
'Twas even you for whom He died.
and gave His life in sacrifice.

For by grace are ye saved through faith; and that not of yourselves: it is the gift of God. (Ephesians 2:8)

For God so loved the world that he gave his only begotten Son, that whosoever believeth in him should not perish, but have everlasting life. For God sent not his Son into the world to condemn the world; but that the world through him might be saved. He that belie-veth on him is not condemned: but he that believeth not is condemned already, because he hath not believed in the name of the only begotten Son of God. And this is the condemnation, that light is come into the world, and men loved darkness rather than light, because their deeds were evil. For every one that doeth evil hateth the light, neither cometh to the light, lest his deeds should be reproved. But he that doeth truth cometh to the light, that his deeds may be made manifest, that they are wrought in God. (John 3:16-21)

And thine ears shall hear a word behind thee, saying: This is the way, walk ye in it, when ye turn to the right hand, and when ye turn to the left. (Isaiah 30:21)

If a man have an hundred sheep, and one of them be gone astray, doth he not leave the ninety and nine, and goeth into the mountains, and seeketh that which is gone astray? And if so be that he find it, verily I say unto you, he rejoiceth more of that sheep, than of the ninety andnine which went not astray. Even so it is not the will of your Father which is in heaven, that one of these little ones should perish. (Matthew 18:12-14)

Behold, I stand at the door, and knock: if any man hear my voice, and open the door, I will come in to him, and will sup with him, and he with me. (Revelation 3:20)

His gentle knock on your heart's door,
you may have even heard before.
He seeks to come and dwell inside;
the only doorknob's on your side.

You need to be concerned
about all that you have learned—
promises that are true,
and what Jesus did for you.

He created all the universe—
wants you with Him to converse—
He's proven that He loves you;
He's waiting to receive you.

You need to hear the Spirit's voice,
then to make the proper choice.
You decide your destiny,
where you will spend eternity.

The Lord is not slack concerning his promise, as some men count slackness; but is longsuffering to us-ward, not willing that any should perish, but that all should come to repentance. (2 Peter 3:9)

In the beginning God created the heaven and the earth. (Genesis 1:1)

In the beginning was the Word, and the Word was with God, and the Word was God. The same was in the beginning with God. All things were made by him; and without him was not anything made that was made. (John 1:1-3)

He was in the world, and the world was made by him, and the world knew him not. He came unto his own, and his own received him not. But as many as received him, to them gave he power to become the sons of God, even to them that believe on his name: Which were born, not of blood, nor of the will of the flesh, nor of the will of man, but of God. And the Word was made flesh, and dwelt among us, (and we beheld his glory, the glory as of the only begotten of the Father, full of grace and truth. (John 1:10-14)

Choose you this day whom ye will serve; whether the gods which your fathers served that were on the other side of the flood, or the gods of the Amorites, in whose land ye dwell: but as for me and my house, we will serve the Lord. (Joshua 24:15b)

No man can serve two masters: for either he will hate the one, and love the other; or else he will hold to the one, and despise the other. Ye cannot serve God and mammon. (Matthew 6:24)

How shall we escape, if we neglect so great salvation? (Hebrews 2:3a)

And choosing to neglect,
the choice that is correct,
takes you down the path
of God's eternal wrath.

Please don't hesitate,
or make Him longer wait.
He'll tell you that He loves you;
His mission is to save you.

One blessing of salvation
is Jesus' preparation
of Heaven's marvelous majesty
where you can spend eternity.

Nay, in all these things we are more than conquerors through him that loved us. For I am persuaded, that neither death, nor life, nor angels, nor principalities, nor powers, nor things present, nor things to come, nor height, nor depth, nor any other creature, shall be able to separate us from the love of God, which is in Christ Jesus our Lord. (Romans 8:37-39)

I have loved you even as the Father has loved me. Live within my love. When you obey me you are living in my love, just as I obey my Father and live in his love. I have told you this so that you will be filled with my joy. Yes, your cup of joy will overflow! (John 15:9-11)

I go to prepare a place for you. And if I go and prepare a place for you, I will come again, and receive you unto myself; that where I am, there ye may be also. (John 14:2b)

Chapter 18

Jesus Loves You

"Jesus loves me this I know
for the Bible tells me so".
The simple words of that chorus
tell us where to look for Jesus.

In that Book you can read
how He'll meet your every need,
by love that gives complete release,
from sins that rob you of your peace.

All that Jesus came to do
was aimed at helping me and you
take the path that we must trod
on our journey that leads to God.

He also gives us His permission
to exercise our free volition
to reject His tender plea,
from our sins to be free.

Attention! This chapter was written in love for the purpose of helping non-believers escape the wrath of God. Sin is damning and will be judged. While we all are guilty and worthy of eternal separation from God, the *Good News is, we can know complete forgiveness!*

Christ's sacrificial death was sufficient for our "justification," which means: "Just as if I'd never sinned." For that to happen on a personal level, we must confess, repent, believe, and obey.

Those are God's requirements. We cannot change them. We either comply or suffer the consequences.

> But my God shall supply all your need according to his riches in glory by Christ Jesus. (Philippians 4:19)

> But God commanded his love toward us, in that, while we were yet sinners, Christ died for us. (Romans 5:8)

> There is therefore now no condemnation to them which are in Christ Jesus, who walk not after the flesh, but after the Spirit. (Romans 8:1)

> I am the Light of the world. So if you follow me, you won't be stumbling through the darkness, for living light will flood your path. (John 8:12, TLB)

> If we live in the Spirit, let us also walk in the Spirit. (Galatians 5:25)

> The thief cometh not, but for to steal, and to kill, and to destroy: I am come that they might have life, and that they might have it more abundantly. (John 10:10)

> For they that are after the flesh do mind the things of the flesh; but they that are after the Spirit the things of the Spirit. For to be carnally minded is death; but to be spiritually minded is life and peace. (Romans 8:5-6)

It's in the heart, the vital place,
where God applies amazing grace.
If the heart is hard, He's turned away;
the consequence then we must pay.

Wherever God has been rejected,
Satan's there to be accepted.
With Christ comes abundant life.
Satan lies and adds to strife.

Despite the path that leads to Heaven,
by His love and mercy given,
many still retain the choice
not to listen to His voice.

To those who make decisions
to reject God's grace provisions,
the result of those abuses
will leave them no excuses.

Wherefore as the Holy Ghost saith, "Today if ye will hear his voice, harden not your hearts. Take heed, brethren, lest there be in any of you an evil heart of unbelief, in departing from the living God. But exhort one another daily, while it is called today; lest any of you be hardened through the deceitfulness of sin. For we are made partakers of Christ, if we hold the beginning of our confidence steadfast unto the end". (Hebrews 3:7-8, 12-14)

Be sober, be vigilant; because your adversary the devil, as a roaring lion, walketh about, seeking whom he may devour. (1 Peter 5:8)

I am come that they might have life, and that they might have it more abundantly. John 10:10b. The thief cometh not, but for to steal, and to kill, and to destroy. (John 10:10a)

...choose for yourselves this day whom you will serve.... But as for me and my household, we will serve the Lord. (Joshua 24:15)

Enter ye in at the strait gate: for wide is the gate, and broad is the way, that leadeth to destruction, and many there be which go in thereat: because strait is the gate, and narrow is the way, which leadeth unto life, and few there be that find it. (Matthew 7:13-14)

The man said, "The woman whom you gave to be with me, she gave me fruit of the tree, and I ate". (Genesis 3:12)

We can choose to sin, of course,
but the outcome's not our choice.
God may cease to chide,
but from judgment, we can't hide.

Everyone, without exception,
compared to God's required perfection,
is worthy of perdition,
with only one escape: redemption.

That miraculous provision
is obtained by our decision
to seek His righteousness
and gain His holiness.

All achieved 'cause Jesus died—
on the Cross was crucified.
Even though we are not good,
our sins are covered by His blood.

For all have sinned, and come short of the glory of God. (Romans 3:23)

He will not always chide: neither will he keep his anger forever. (Psalm 103:9)

It is appointed unto men once to die, but after that the judgment. (Hebrews 9:27)

No one is good—no one in all the world is innocent. No one anywhere has kept on doing what is right; not one. (Romans 3:10b, 12b, TLB)

Be ye therefore perfect, even as your Father which is in heaven is perfect. (Matthew 5:48)

Fear not: for I have redeemed thee, I have called thee by thy name; thou art mine. (Isaiah 43:1)

Behold, what manner of love the Father hath bestowed upon us.... Beloved, now are we the sons of God, and it doth not yet appear what we shall be: but we know that, when he shall appear, we shall be like him; for we shall see him as he is. And every man that hath this hope in him purifieth himself, even as he is pure. (1 John 3:1-3, TLB)

But seek ye first the kingdom of God, and his righteousness; and all these things shall be added unto you. (Matthew 6:33)

For there is not a just man upon earth, that doeth good, and sinneth not. (Ecclesiastes 7:20)

For this is my blood of the covenant, which is poured out for many for the forgiveness of sins. (Matthew 26:28)

When we face reality,
all of us are guilty.
Saints are covered by insurance;
God's forgiveness their assurance.

That's the beauty of God's Plan,
on our goodness, we don't depend!
It's the Great I Am in whom we trust.
He's the One who died for us.

As far as East is from West,
that's where our sins are cast.
They're buried in the deepest sea,
never again, for Him to see.

Our sins are not remembered,
nor on us again encumbered,
when we have done our part,
and He has cleansed our heart.

But isn't this unfair for God to let criminals go free, and say that they are innocent? No, for he does it on the basis of their trust in Jesus who took away their sins. (Romans 3:26b, TLB)

All the world stands hushed and guilty before Almighty God. (Romans 3:19b, TLB)

But, now God has shown us a different way to heaven—not by "being good enough" and trying to keep his laws, but by a new way. Now God says he will accept and acquit us—declare us "not guilty"—if we trust Jesus Christ to take away our sins. (Romans 3:21-22a, TLB)

He has removed our sins as far away from us as the east is from the west. (Psalm 103:12)

You will tread our sins beneath your feet; you will throw them into the depths of the ocean! (Micah 7:19b, TLB)

I, yes, I alone am he who blots away your sins for my own sake and will never think of them again. (Isaiah 43:25)

Have mercy upon me, O God, according to thy loving kindness: according unto the multitude of thy tender mercies blot out my transgressions. Wash me thoroughly from mine iniquity, and cleanse me from my sin. (Psalm 51:1-2)

When you are judged on Judgment Day,
will your debt be yet to pay?
Or will the Book of Life record
your name and deeds and earned reward?

There is no greater earthly goal
than doing all to save your soul.
God loved enough to give His Son
so you could live when life is done.

If right now you're bound by sin
and have not yet accepted Him,
please listen to His voice;
*He's **urging** you to make that choice!*

While you are able still to choose,
you'd be so foolish to refuse.
If to His call you fail to yield,
your own doom you will have sealed!

You saw me before I was born and scheduled each day of my life before I began to breathe. Every day was recorded in your book! (Psalm 139:16, TLB)

For we must all stand before Christ to be judged and have our lives laid bare—before him. Each of us will receive whatever he deserves for the good or bad things he has done in his earthly body. (2 Corinthians 5:10).

Then another book was opened, which is the book of life. And the dead were judged by what was written in the books, according to what they had done. (Revelation 20:12)

For what doth it profit a man, if he gain the whole world, and suffer the loss of his own soul? Or what exchange shall a man give for his soul? (Matthew 16:26)

For God so loved the world, that he gave his only begotten Son, that whosoever believeth in him should not perish, but have everlasting life. (John 3:16)

Choose you this day whom ye will serve. (Joshua 15:16a)

How shall we escape, if we neglect so great salvation? (Hebrews 2:3)

For God sent not his Son into the world to condemn the world; but that the world through him might be saved. He that believeth on him is not condemned: but he that believeth not is condemned already, because he hath not believed in the name of the only begotten Son of God. (John 3:17-18)

If in your heart a battle's raging,
it's one that God "in love" is waging,
to shield you from demonic forces,
saving you from damning choices.

You, yourself, now hold the key,
to eternal death or victory!
What action steps must you take
to ensure a fast and clean escape?

Find the page of "My Confession"!
Pray the prayer for your salvation.
God will prove that He is real,
through joy and hope, He will reveal.

For when you do confess your sins
and know that He then reigns within,
your faith will bring the revelation:
you are in Christ a new creation.

There hath no temptation taken you but such as is common to man: but God is faithful, who will not suffer (allow) you to be tempted above that ye are able; but will with the temptation also make a way to escape, that ye may be able to bear it. (1 Corinthians 10:13)

Let no man say when he is tempted, I am tempted of God: for God cannot be tempted with evil, neither tempteth he any man: But every man is tempted, when he is drawn away of his own lust, and enticed. Then when lust hath conceived, it bringeth forth sin: and sin, when it is finished, bringeth forth death. (James 1:13-15)

Blessed is the man that endureth temptation: for when he is tried, he shall receive the crown of life, which the Lord hath promised to them that love him. (James 1:12).

Create in me a clean heart, O God; and renew a right spirit within me. Restore unto me the joy of thy salvation. The sacrifices of God are a broken spirit: a broken and a contrite heart, O God, thou wilt not despise. (Psalm 51:10, 12a, 17)

Therefore if any man be in Christ, he is a new creature: old things are passed away; behold, all things are become new. For he hath made him to be sin for us, who knew no sin; that we might be made the righteousness of God in him. (2 Corinthians 5:17, 21)

That fact of faith brings such release;
no other source can match its peace.
When God, the Comforter, in you abides,
your sinful heart is justified.

And if you walk in His pure Light,
obey His Word and do what's right,
you'll be one within the crowd
that meets Jesus in the cloud.

Therefore being justified by faith, we have peace with God through our Lord Jesus Christ: By whom also we have access by faith into this grace wherein we stand, and rejoice in hope of the glory of God. (Romans 5:1-2)

Peace I leave with you, my peace I give unto you: not as the world giveth, give I unto you. Let not your heart be troubled, neither let it be afraid. (John 14:27)

But I will send you the Comforter—the Holy Spirit, the source of all truth. He will come to you from the Father and will tell you all about me. Now the God of peace, that brought again from the dead our Lord Jesus, that great shepherd of the sheep, through the blood of the everlasting covenant, make you perfect in every good work to do his will, working in you that which is well-pleasing in his sight, through Jesus Christ; to whom be glory for ever and ever. Amen. (John 15:19b-21)

But if we walk in the light, as he is in the light, we have fellowship with one another, and the blood of Jesus his Son cleanses us from all sin. (1 John 1:7)

Chapter 19

Jesus' Gift

Who is this One who makes the claim:
He paid the price for sin and shame?
He's the Savior, whom God sent
to cleanse my heart when I repent.

I believe He is God's Son,
and He is the Only One,
who has the power to save
and free me from the grave.

I believe He died for me.
His love included me.
My sins were on that tree.
His grace extends to me.

Jesus is His name,
and He took all the blame,
for sins that we commit,
which we to Him submit.

The poetry speaks for itself. It points to many Scriptures that reflect the content of the poetry.

> Behold the Lamb of God, which taketh away the sin of the world. (John 1:29)

> For God so loved the world, that he gave his only begotten Son, that whosoever believeth in him should not perish, but have everlasting life. (John 3:16)

> Except you repent, you shall all likewise perish. (Luke 13:5)

> And I saw, and bare record that this is the Son of God. (John 1:34)

> Jesus saith unto him, "I am the way, the truth, and the life: no man cometh unto the Father, but by me". (John 14:6)

> For the wages of sin is death, but the free gift of God is eternal life in Christ Jesus our Lord. (Romans 6:23)

> Who his own self bare our sins in his own body on the tree that we, being dead to sins, should live unto righteousness: by whose stripes you were healed. (1 Peter 2:24)

> There is therefore now no condemnation to them which are in Christ Jesus, who walk not after the flesh, but after the Spirit. (Romans 8:1)

> For by grace are ye saved through faith; and that not of yourselves: it is the gift of God: not of works, lest any man should boast. (Ephesians 2:8-9)

> But he was wounded for our transgressions; he was crushed for our iniquities; upon him was the chastisement that brought us peace, and with his stripes we are healed. (Isaiah 53:5)

I repented of my sins
and gave them all to Him.
From every sin I'm free.
His blood is cleansing me.

The promise He now gives
to all whom He forgives—
eternal life is free;
He gave that gift to me!

It's a gift I did not earn,
and one I did not spurn.
It's yours also to receive,
when you, too, believe!

Is your name now written
in the Book of Life in Heaven?
Has Jesus' blood blotted out
every sin and every doubt?

I acknowledged my sin to You, and my iniquity I did not hide; I said, "I will confess my transgressions to the LORD", and You forgave the guilt of my sin. (Psalm 32:5)

The blood of Jesus Christ his Son cleanseth us from all sin. (1 John 1:7b)

Then what can we boast about doing to earn our salvation? Nothing at all. Why? Because our acquittal is not based on our good deeds; it is based on what Christ has done and our faith in him. So it is that we are saved by faith in Christ and not by the good things we do. (Romans 3:27-28, TLB)

If we confess our sins, he is faithful and just to forgive us our sins, and to cleanse us from all unrighteousness. (1 John 1:9)

And they said, "Believe on the Lord Jesus Christ, and thou shalt be saved...". (Acts 16:31a)

Ye have not chosen me, but I have chosen you, and ordained you, that ye should go and bring forth fruit, and *that* your fruit should remain: that whatsoever ye shall ask of the Father in my name, he may give it you. (John 15:16)

And they overcame him (Satan) by the blood of the Lamb, and by the word of their testimony... (Revelation 12:11a)

And the Spirit and the bride say, Come. And let him that heareth say, Come. And let him that is athirst come. And whosoever will, let him take the water of life freely. (Revelation 22:17)

For whosoever shall call upon the name of the Lord shall be saved. (Romans 10:13)

If you refuse His gift that's free,
and in your heart do not believe,
then you reject His love and grace,
and God's judgment you must face.

When you stand before God's throne,
in His Presence all alone,
He will see your sin and doubt,
where your name is blotted out.

If His mercy is rejected,
then your soul is not protected.
You cannot choose, not to choose.
With Jesus, win! With Satan, lose!

Is it worth the fleeting pleasure
that keeps your soul from bliss forever?
Must you still retain control,
with stubborn heart that costs your soul?

The one who rejects me and does not receive my words has a judge; the word that I have spoken will judge him on the last day. (John 12:48)

Whoever believes in him is not condemned, but whoever does not believe is condemned already, because he has not believed in the name of the only Son of God. And this is the judgment: the light has come into the world, and people loved the darkness rather than the light because their works were evil. (John 3:18-19)

And I saw the dead, small and great, stand before God; and the books were opened: and another book was opened, which is the book of life: and the dead were judged out of those things which were written in the books, according to their works. (Revelation 20:12)

And whosoever was not found written in the book of life was cast into the lake of fire. (Revelation 20:15)

Therefore God sends them a strong delusion, so that they may believe what is false, in order that all may be condemned who did not believe the truth but had pleasure in unrighteousness. (2 Thessalonians 2:11-12)

The one who rejects me and does not receive my words has a judge; the word that I have spoken will judge him on the last day. (John 12:48)

Whoever believes in the Son has eternal life; whoever does not obey the Son shall not see life, but the wrath of God remains on him. (John 3:36)

And if you choose to just neglect,
"The Jesus Way" that is correct,
then you seal your own doom;
for you, God's Heaven has no room.

For if the word spoken through angels proved unalterable, and every transgression and disobedience received a just penalty, how will we escape if we neglect so great a salvation? (Hebrews 2:2-3a)

Chapter 20

Heaven

Heaven's great majestic grandeur
exceeds by far imagined wonder.
Its beauty none can comprehend
and then with words enlighten men.

Time and peace never cease,
and joy and love are both increased,
and every "sense" of human pleasure
is magnified beyond all measure.

God Himself is radiant Light,
and where He is, there is no night.
We never cease to be amazed;
there is no end to songs of praise.

How sweet it is the music blends.
Angels hover on waves it rends.
Glorious marvels of Heaven's splendor,
we see and hear and feel forever.

Words are inadequate to convey the perception of value experienced by those who know they are ready for Heaven. Jesus gave His life to give us eternal life. That level of love will never be equaled, and nothing compares with the level of peace and serenity that comes from a personal relationship with the Savior.

> Eye hath not seen, nor ear heard, neither have entered into the heart of man, the things which God hath prepared for them that love him. (1 Corinthians 2:9)

> And the city had no need of the sun, neither of the moon, to shine in it: for the glory of God did lighten it, and the Lamb is the light thereof. (Revelation 21:23)

> And there shall be no night there; and they need no candle, neither light of the sun; for the Lord God giveth them light: and they shall reign for ever and ever. (Revelation 22:5)

> And I heard as it were the voice of a great multitude, and as the voice of many waters, and as the voice of mighty thunderings, saying, Alleluia: for the Lord God omnipotent reigneth. Let us be glad and rejoice, and give honor to him: for the marriage of the Lamb is come, and his wife hath made herself ready. And to her was granted that she should be arrayed in fine linen, clean and white: for the fine linen is the righteousness of saints. (Revelation 19:6-8)

Chapter 21

My Confession

When Jesus bore that heavy Cross,
its weight was sins for all the lost.
I feel ashamed, my sins were there;
He cared enough, their weight to bear.

His love was on display that day;
He gave His life my debt to pay.
His mercy now extends to you;
receive it with all gratitude.

Take one step toward Him;
He'll extend to you His hand,
then lead you all the way
to a place where you can pray.

Cry out to God with true confession.
He'll accept your heart's sincere contrition.
You need do nothing to prepare.
He wants you, "Just as you are"!

Just As I Am

Just as I am, without one plea
But that Thy blood was she'd for me
And that Thou bidd'st me come to Thee,
O Lamb of God, I come, I come.

Just as I am and waiting not
To rid my soul of one dark blot,
To Thee, whose blood can cleanse each spot,
O Lamb of God, I come, I come.

Just as I am, though tossed about
With many a conflict, many a doubt,
Fightings and fears within, without,
O Lamb of God, I come, I come.

Just as I am, poor, wretched, blind;
Sight, riches, healing of the mind,
Yea, all I need, in Thee to find,
O Lamb of God, I come, I come.

Just as I am, Thou wilt receive,
Wilt welcome, pardon, cleanse, relieve;
Because Thy promise I believe,
O Lamb of God, I come, I come.

Just as I am, Thy love unknown
Has broken every barrier down.
Now to be Thine, yea, Thine alone,
O Lamb of God, I come, I come.

I will never in a thousand years
forget the day I shed my tears.
I reached out and took His hand;
that moment my new life began.

Jesus stayed to help me pray,
even gave me words to say.
And at the very start,
He touched and broke my heart.

He'll do the same for you,
if you ask Him to.
I started out confessing,
and that turned into blessing.

What He asked me to do,
applies as well to you.
If like me, you came to pray,
repeat the words He helped me say.

The verses that follow are David's confession and plea for mercy and forgiveness for his sins. They opened a window to his heart. He was humbled, repentant, and contrite.

God knows our thoughts and the intentions of our heart. We cannot fool Him. Clearly, David was sincere in his prayer, and God heard it and answered with forgiveness.

> Create in me a clean heart, O God; and renew a right spirit within me.
>
> Cast me not away from thy presence; and take not thy holy spirit from me.
>
> Restore unto me the joy of thy salvation; and uphold me with thy free spirit.
>
> Then will I teach transgressors thy ways; and sinners shall be converted unto thee.
>
> Deliver me from blood guiltiness, O God, thou God of my salvation: and my tongue shall sing aloud of thy righteousness.
>
> O Lord, open thou my lips; and my mouth shall shew forth thy praise.
>
> For thou desirest not sacrifice; else would I give it: thou delightest not in burnt offering.
>
> The sacrifices of God are a broken spirit: a broken and a contrite heart, O God, thou wilt not despise. (Psalm 51:10-17)

I humbly bowed my head,
and this is what I said:
"Dear Jesus, where do I begin,
so many times I've sinned?

All I know to do
is give them all to you.
So Jesus, cleanse my heart,
let every sin depart.

I'm begging your forgiveness
in sincere and true repentance.
My heart's door now is open,
and you are more than welcome.

I believe You are God's Son;
You are the Only One,
who can forgive my sins
and make me clean within.

When we humble ourselves in submission to God, the power of the Holy Spirit is released. What begins with humility and submission ends in domination and victory over the most powerful force of evil that ever existed, Satan.

God resists the proud, but gives grace to the humble. Submit yourselves therefore to God. Resist the devil, and he will flee from you. (James 4:6-7)

For the LORD takes pleasure in his people; he adorns the humble with salvation. (Psalm 149:4)

Behold, I stand at the door, and knock: if any man hear my voice, and open the door, I will come in to him, and will sup [fellowship] with him, and he with me. (Revelation 3:20)

I acknowledged my sin to you, and I did not cover my iniquity; I said, "I will confess my transgressions to the Lord," and you forgave the iniquity of my sin. (Psalm 32:5)

Create in me a clean heart, O God; and renew a right spirit within me. Purge me with hyssop, and I shall be clean: wash me, and I shall be whiter than snow. (Psalm 51:10, 7)

Repent ye therefore, and be converted, that your sins may be blotted out, when the times of refreshing shall come from the presence of the Lord. (Acts 3:19)

If we confess our sins, he is faithful and just to forgive us our sins, and to cleanse us from all unrighteousness. (1 John 1:9)

Neither is there salvation in any other: for there is none other name under heaven given among men, whereby we must be saved. (Acts 4:12)

By faith I do believe
that, in fact, I have received,
a brand new perfect heart;
a new life today I start.

Thank you for your promise,
and thank you for forgiveness.
I now know what to do;
"I will follow you"!

Please help me to obey.
Give me strength each day.
Keep me in the Way.
In Jesus Name I pray.
Amen!

The order of confession is: repent, receive, believe, share (tell others what Christ did for you).

> For you are all the children of God by faith in Christ Jesus. (Galatians 3:26)

> A new heart also will I give you, and a new spirit will I put within you. (Ezekiel 36:26a)

> Your old evil desires were nailed to the cross with him. And since your old sin-loving nature "died" with Christ, we know that you will share his new life. (Romans 6:6a, 8, TLB)

> If the Son therefore shall make you free, ye shall be free indeed. (John 8:36)

> Christ rose from the dead and will never die again. Death no longer has any power over him. He died once for all to end sin's power, but now he lives forever in unbroken fellowship with God. (Romans 6:9-11, TLB)

> My sheep hear my voice, and I know them, and they follow me: And I give unto them eternal life; and they shall never perish, neither shall any man pluck them out of my hand. (John 10:27-28)

> For all the promises of God find their Yea in him. That is why it is through him that we utter our Amen to God for his glory. (2 Corinthians 1:20)

Chapter 22

Jesus as Your Savior

The prayer you prayed of true confession,
Jesus answered with compassion.
Of all the sins that you've committed
you now know that you're acquitted!

Now that Jesus is your Savior,
many blessings you can savor.
Give Him thanks a thousand ways;
honor Him with all your praise.

You need to know, of course,
your life has changed its course.
You've begun a new relationship;
with God you now have fellowship.

What is it you can do
to grow His Life in you?
Thank Him when you pray,
and do that every day.

The poems to this point were written to climax with "My Confession". If you prayed that prayer with sincerity and believe in your heart that you are forgiven, then you are forgiven. You see, Jesus forgave you when He died for you. Your sins were paid for by His blood. All He asks of you is to believe that! So give Him thanks! As understanding sinks in, the awareness of peace and blessing will follow.

> And he is the propitiation (the atoning sacrifice) for our sins: and not for ours only, but also for the sins of the whole world. (1 John 2:2)

> The eyes of the Lord search back and forth across the whole earth, looking for people whose hearts are perfect toward him, so that he can show his great power in helping them. (2 Chronicles 16:9, TLB)

> I pray that you will begin to understand how incredibly great his power is to help those who believe him. It is that same mighty power that raised Christ from the dead and seated him in the place of honor at God's right hand in heaven. (Ephesians 1:19-20, TLB)

> Whoso offereth praise glorifieth [honoreth] me. (Psalm 50:23a)

> The Holy Spirit helps us with our daily problems and in our praying. For we don't even know what we should pray for nor how to pray as we should, but the Holy Spirit prays for us with such feeling that it cannot be expressed in words. And the Father who knows all hearts knows, of course, what the Spirit is saying as he pleads for us in harmony with God's own will. (Romans 8:26-27, TLB)

> Let your lives overflow with joy and thanksgiving for all he has done. (Colossians 2:7b)

Then ask to know His will,
which He's eager to fulfill.
Look daily to His Word.
That's where His voice is heard.

Make His will your heart's desire,
so you will do what He requires.
He wants to feel your love each day,
and that He does when you obey.

Blessings flow from what you've done,
accepting Jesus, God's dear Son.
You now can face Him unafraid;
your debt for sin has all been paid.

A race is now for you to run;
a prize to gain when you are done.
Seek Him first in all you do;
His righteousness He'll give to you.

Now just as you trusted Christ to save you, trust him, too, for each day's problems; live in vital union with him. Let your roots grow down into him and draw up nourishment from him. See that you go on growing in the Lord, and become strong and vigorous in the truth you were taught. (Colossians. 2:6-7a)

Trust in the Lord with all thine heart; and lean not unto thine own understanding. In all thy ways acknowledge him, and he shall direct thy paths. (Proverbs 3:5-6)

And this is the confidence that we have in him, that, if we ask any thing according to his will, he heareth us: And if we know that he hear us, whatsoever we ask, we know that we have the petitions that we desired of him. (1 John 5:14-15)

Let us therefore come boldly to the throne of grace, that we may obtain mercy and find grace to help in time of need. (Hebrews 4:16)

Ask, and it shall be given you; seek, and ye shall find; knock, and it shall be opened unto you: For every one that asketh receiveth; and he that seeketh findeth; and to him that knocketh it shall be opened. (Matthew 7:7-8)

Delight thyself also in the Lord: and he shall give thee the desires of thine heart. Commit thy way unto the Lord; trust also in him; and he shall bring it to pass. (Psalm 37:4-5)

For there is only one God and one Mediator who can reconcile God and humanity—the man Christ Jesus. He gave his life to purchase freedom for everyone. (1 Timothy 2:5-6a, NLT)

Blessed is the man that endureth temptation: for when he is tried, he shall receive the crown of life, which the Lord hath promised to them that love him. (James 1:12)

The Holy Spirit will be your guide.
His voice will help when you decide,
on matters where you hesitate,
not certain of the path to take.

What that means is this:
you now have easy access
to Almighty God, the source,
your all-knowing, wise resource.

He says He'll never leave you,
never once forsake you.
He wants you though to ask Him
every time you need Him.

When temptations come along,
they help to make you strong.
The more that you resist,
the less Satan will persist.

Know ye not that your body is the temple of the Holy Ghost which is in you…. (2 Corinthians 6:19a)

And thine ears shall hear a word behind thee, saying, This is the way, walk ye in it, when ye turn to the right hand, and when ye turn to the left. (Isaiah 30:21)

If God be for us, who can be against us? (Romans 8:31)

I can do all things through Christ which strengtheneth me. (Philippians 4:13)

But Jesus beheld them, and said unto them, "With men this is impossible; but with God all things are possible". (Matthew 19:26)

He hath said: "I will never leave thee, nor forsake thee". (Hebrews 13:5b)

If any of you lack wisdom, let him ask of God, that giveth to all men liberally, and upbraideth not; and it shall be given him. (James 1:5)

There hath no temptation taken you but such as is common to man: but God is faithful, who will not suffer [allow] you to be tempted above that ye are able; but will with the temptation also make a way to escape, that ye may be able to bear it. (2 Corinthians 10:13)

Flee also youthful lusts: but follow righteousness, faith, charity, peace, with them that call on the Lord out of a pure heart. (2 Timothy 2:22)

Submit yourselves therefore to God. Resist the devil, and he will flee from you. (James 4:7)

God gives armor for defense:
His Word's a sword for offense;
you have a helmet of salvation;
shoes that walk His Proclamations.

Your breastplate is righteousness;
your belt secures truthfulness;
by your steady shield of faith,
arrows miss each vital place.

God's Word is always right;
it's now your source of light.
Your friends, it too can guide;
it's yours to share, not hide.

The best way you can grow:
let your friends and others know,
what Jesus means to you,
so they can know Him, too.

Wherefore take unto you the whole armor of God that ye may be able to withstand in the evil day, and having done all, to stand. (Ephesians 6:13)

Stand therefore, having your loins girt about with truth, and having on the breastplate of righteousness. (Ephesians 6:14)

And your feet shod with the preparation of the gospel of peace. (Ephesians 6:15)

Above all, taking the shield of faith, wherewith ye shall be able to quench all the fiery darts of the wicked. (Ephesians 6:16)

And take the helmet of salvation, and the sword of the Spirit, which is the word of God. (Ephesians 6:17)

But as many as received him, to them gave he power to become the sons of God, even to them that believe on his name. (John 1:12)

Neither do men light a candle and put it under a bushel, but on a candlestick, and it gives light unto all that are in the house. (Matthew 5:15)

Let your light so shine before men, that they may see your good works, and glorify your Father which is in heaven. (Matthew 5:16)

And for me, that utterance may be given unto me, that I may open my mouth boldly, to make known the mystery of the gospel, For which I am an ambassador in bonds: that therein I may speak boldly, as I ought to speak. (Ephesians 6:19-20)

For I am not ashamed of the gospel of Christ: for it is the power of God unto salvation to everyone that believeth. (Romans 1:16)

Chapter 23

Prophecy Real Time

When whatever God requires
is the same as our desires,
He protects from Satan's lies,
giving us abundant life.

If His Word that we receive,
we change, reject, or don't believe,
or His commandments we reverse,
He says there'll be a curse.

When we defy God's Truth and Light,
the darkness hides the "right" from "sight".
Satan's lies are soon believed,
and then we learn, we've been deceived.

All who follow Satan's path,
will have to face God's awful wrath.
What they sew, they will reap;
every promise, God will keep.

God desires to be magnified in our lives, not diminished. He wants to give us our desires and He does that when they are in harmony with His will.

> Delight thyself also in the LORD: and he shall give thee the desires of thine heart. (Psalm 37:4)

Satan's goal is to steal, deceive, kill, and destroy; Jesus came to bring abundant life

> The thief cometh not, but for to steal, and to kill, and to destroy: I am come that they might have life, and that they might have it more abundantly. (John 10:10)

God is very clear about the severe consequences to any and all who try to make His Word say something He did not intend for it to say, or to add to it, or delete parts from it.

> As we said before, so say it now again, if any man preach any other gospel unto you than that ye have received, let him be accursed. (Galatians 1:9)

> Add thou not unto his words, lest he reprove thee, and thou be found a liar. (Proverbs 30:6)

Light and darkness cannot exist together. Light dispels the darkness, but as soon as it is extinguished, darkness returns.

> The light of the body is the eye: if therefore thine eye be single, thy whole body shall be full of light. But if thine eye be evil, thy whole body shall be full of darkness. If therefore the light that is in thee be darkness, how great is that darkness! (Matthew 6:21-22)

> *Be not deceived, God is not mocked; for whatsoever a man soweth, that shall he also reap. For he that soweth to his flesh shall of the flesh reap corruption.* **(Galatians 6:6-7)**

It is a sad and solemn day,
we are compelled to have to say,
the highest Court in our dear land
has ruled against what God commands.

By that ruling the Court erased
Laws of God that saints embrace.
Now every day that news is cast,
more prophecies are come to pass.

Five Justices have just revised
the marriage Laws that God devised.
But human laws cannot rescind,
God's judgment that will now begin.

God said when good is vilified,
and sins instead are glorified,
His Light will lose its glow,
and be replaced with "woe".

Prophecy Real Time Number 1

June 26, 2015, will go down in history as a day of infamy for America.

The most significant offense of the ruling is the fact that the Court attributed to itself authority superior to the authority of God.

God defined marriage as a covenant between one man and one woman for the purpose of intimate love-making, sexual pleasure, and procreation, all of which He honors and blesses.

> So God created man in his own image, in the image of God he created him; male and female created them. And God blessed and God said unto them, Be fruitful, and multiply, and replenish the earth. (Genesis 1:27-28a)

It is unrealistic to think the Justices did not know what the Bible says about marriage, sexual immorality, and homosexuality. They knew! Yet, those who favored the ruling proved by their vote, they do not believe in the truthfulness of God's Word, nor in the promised consequences for violating it.

> When they knew God, they glorified him not as God, neither were thankful; but became vain in their imaginations, and their foolish heart was darkened. Professing themselves to be wise, they became fools. (Romans 1:22)

> Woe unto them that are wise in their own eyes, and prudent in their own sight! (Isaiah 5:21)

The ruling was an overt act of defiance toward God.

> Woe unto them that call evil good, and good evil; that put darkness for light, and light for darkness; that put bitter for sweet, and sweet for bitter! (Isaiah 5:20)

While the ruling may give solace to homosexual male couples and female couples, whose lust for each other overcomes their

Five Justices became superior,
rendering God to them inferior;
they put themselves upon the throne
that God demands is His alone.

Will God ignore their arrogance
for which He has no tolerance?
Will "justice" still be just?
In whom do we "now" trust?

From history past, by recollection,
we see prophetic repetition —
sins of Sodom and Gomorrah
will be rampant here tomorrow.

For every sin that is immoral
is in fact a Truth denial.
With this legal liberation,
there's less moral hesitation.

self-control, the Justices in the majority now are complicit in the eternal damnation of the same people they presumed to liberate.

> The Lord hath prepared his throne in the heavens; and
> his kingdom ruleth over all. (Psalm 103:19)

The SCOTUS ruling does far more than legalize same-sex marriage. The ruling gives anyone who is inclined to do so all the excuse they need to engage in immoral-sex, with impunity. It also gives license to singles to engage in homosexuality by diminishing the social barriers that have existed since the nation was founded.

While sex within marriage between one man and one woman is honorable and good, God judges sexual immorality and homosexuality, harshly. They violate and defile what God intended to be sacred.

> Flee from sexual immorality. Every other sin a person
> commits is outside the body, but the sexually immoral
> person sins against his own body. (1 Corinthians
> 6:18, TLB)

> Don't fool yourselves—those who live immoral
> lives, who are idol worshipers, adulterers or homo-
> sexuals—will have no share in his Kingdom. (1
> Corinthians 6:9, TLB)

The LGBT community has a problem. Its members not only want to continue in their sin, they want to be exonerated from the scourge of wrong doing without a change of heart or behavior. *That will not work!*

> And he said to them all, if any man will come after
> me, let him deny himself, and take up his cross daily,
> and follow me. (Luke 9:23)

Straight men and women are attracted to the opposite sex, but that is never an excuse for them to be immoral in their behavior.

So the marriage of two men,
or two women joined in sin,
is now honored and respected
and is legally protected.

But the Court cannot control
the destruction of the soul.
Sin will seal their awful fate,
when God declares them "reprobate".

Those sexual deviations
are in the end "beyond salvation".
God's wrath they then must face,
when He withdraws His grace.

America will be destroyed;
God's arsenal will be employed.
Like Sodom and Gomorrah
here today and gone tomorrow!

sex drive is strong and requires self-control. But, just because the attraction and drive are biological realities does not mean people have to act on them. But there is a way out. The Bible says:

> There hath *no temptation* taken you but such as is common to man: but God is faithful, who will not suffer (allow) you to be tempted above that ye are able; but will with the temptation also make a way to escape, that ye may be able to bear it. (1 Corinthians 10:13)

Those are the *necessary* and *sufficient* steps to becoming a child of God and receiving the gift of eternal life.

Readers should take note of the fact that finding the *truth* requires meeting *necessary* and *sufficient* conditions, whether the search is through *faith,* spiritually, or *facts,* scientifically.

Clearly, God wants the *Truth* to be manifest *in love* in every life. The time for doing that is short, very short. That is a reality confirmed by God's Word and End-Time, factual, prophetic fulfillments, and *God does not lie!*

That is why America needs to be alerted to the consequences of the ruling by the majority Justices:

> For this cause God gave them up unto vile affections: for even their women did change the natural use into that which is against nature. And likewise also the men, leaving the natural use of the woman, burned in their lust one toward another; men with men working that which is unseemly, and receiving in themselves that recompense of their error which was meet. And even as they did not like to retain God in their knowledge, God gave them over to a *reprobate* mind, to do those things which are not convenient; (Romans 1:26-28)

In context the word *"reprobate"* means *"beyond salvation"*.

> Thou shalt not lie with mankind, as with womankind: it is abomination. (Leviticus 18:22)

How will that come to be
that awful certainty?
And when can we expect
that judgment God affects?

Through science we can show,
by facts that we now know,
time is running out,
and Truth is speaking out.

By formulae we derived,
from what prophets prophesied,
three dates could be the keys
to important prophecies.

The dates of those events
are Feast Days of Atonement.
The first arrives this very September;
a month we likely will remember.

The Word could not be clearer! Homosexual marriage and the homosexual lifestyle are sins that God will judge. God refers to them as abominations and promises to judge them.

Prophecy Real Time Number 2

So what does the ruling by SCOTUS predict for America? Well, for the same sins, God *destroyed* Sodom and Gomorrah.

Two verses summarize God's judgment on the two cities and the area surrounding them. The complete account is recorded in Genesis 19. In the first verse two angels told Lot to get himself and his family out of town, because they were sent by God to destroy the place.

> For we will destroy the city completely. The stench of the place has reached to heaven and God has sent us to destroy it. (Genesis 19:13, TLB)

Lot and his family fled, and God kept His Word:

> *Then the Lord rained down fire and flaming tar from heaven upon Sodom and Gomorrah, and utterly destroyed them,* along with the other cities and villages of the plain, eliminating all life — people, plants, and animals alike. (Genesis 19:24-25, TLB)

We do not want to convey to readers the idea that God has a schedule to follow and we have figured it out. We do not know *precisely when* God will pour out His wrath in judgment on America.

While God does not identify the day nor the hour, He does provide plenty of evidence that the day is approaching, and He expects His followers to make themselves aware of that general time frame.

> When it is evening, ye say, it will be fair weather: for the sky is red. And in the morning, it will be foul weather today: for the sky is red and lowering. O ye hypocrites, ye can discern the face of the sky; but *can ye not discern the signs of the times?* (Matthew 16:3-4)

Before or during Tribulation,
we'll see the actual devastation,
and the evidence we have seen
points to twenty seventeen.

So we into the future back
to watch our faith turn into fact.
For every promise will come true,
those yet to be and those in view.

Where's the proof, they're not to be,
when light is shed on history?
Be not deceived that these events
can be explained: "Coincidence"!

Could it be there's no escape;
we've crossed the line and it's too late,
and this judicial travesty
steals our place in history?

We do not want to put God in a box, but conditions at this point are optimal for significant events to take place.

For example a meltdown of the US and global economies could take place at any time.

In the past seven years, the national debt has grown from $13.6 trillion to $18 trillion, and many economists say that is unsustainable, a crash is inevitable.

September 2015 closes out a Shemitah/Sabbatical year (seven years), a Shemitah/Sabbatical week of years (49 years), and the *tenth* 490 year cycle.

Readers need to know that the greatest nation in human history is absent, in biblical references, during the greatest concentration of prophetic fulfillments in human history.

The silence from that absence is deafening! Something obviously happens that renders America impotent and non-threatening prior to the time when major End-Time wars and other events take place.

Let's consider some possibilities.

The poetry highlights several "Could it be's". The facts are that all of those conditions exist to some degree now. Ultimately, when God's wrath is fully poured out, it will be quick and thorough. America will be caught off guard; we will not see it coming; we will not be able to defend ourselves.

We are living in *the* most perilous time in our history, which is a prophetically observable condition of the last days.

> This know also, that in the last days perilous times shall come. (2 Timothy 3:1)

> But evil men and seducers shall wax worse and worse deceiving and being deceived. (2 Timothy 3:13)

> So do these also resist the truth: men of corrupt minds, reprobate concerning the faith. *But they shall proceed no further:* for their folly shall be manifest unto all men. (2 Timothy 3:8a-9a)

> The Lord hath opened his armory, and hath brought forth the *weapons of his indignation.* (Jeremiah 50:25)

183

Could it be our debt increases
so the value of the dollar ceases,
causing chaos and disorder
that bring about a New World Order?

Could it be by persecution
recorded in the Revelation?
Even now the culture's hostile
to true Believers and the Gospel?

Could it be from hate and crime,
God said would come at end of time,
or perhaps from lack of will
to defend ourselves from those who kill?

Could it be from new disease,
carried by the wind or breeze,
or from a house that cannot stand,
because we built it on the sand?

O pleasure-mad kingdom (America), living at ease (America), bragging as the greatest in the world—(America) listen to the sentence of my court upon your sins. (Isaiah 47:8a, TLB)

Sit in darkness and silence. . . (Isaiah 47:5a, TLB)

Your "wisdom" and "knowledge" have caused you to turn away from me and *claim that you yourself are Jehovah (Justice's ruling). That is why disaster shall overtake you suddenly—so suddenly that you won't know where it comes from.* And there will be no atonement then to cleanse away your sins. (Isaiah 47:10-11, TLB)

Prophecy Real Time Number 3

In keeping with the theme of the present Chapter, we summarize three prophecies that are partially fulfilled and predicted to be completely fulfilled within a decade from this writing, hence the reference to "real time."

Here is a head's up!

In order to make the final points in this segment, we need to report many details. Bear with us, because those details are critically relevant to events in America's immediate future. Those events identify the most significant time in the history of mankind, as you shall see.

God thought the seventh day was so important as a day of rest that He took that day off Himself. On the seventh day of creation, He rested.

Then when He gave Moses the Ten Commandments, the seventh day became the Sabbath, which He commanded to be a time for rest, restoration, refreshing, and refocusing. That day also equates justice with forgiveness and reconciliation. However, if punishment is deserved, judgment is meted out, as well.

Thus, the seventh day of every week is a Sabbath. Every seventh year is a Sabbath year, also called a Sabbatical year. Every seventh Sabbatical year (49 years) is a Sabbatical week of years. Every

185

Could it be that in our pride,
what God says is set aside,
then men decide what's good and wise,
and that's the cause of our demise?

Could it be our leaders fail
to give support to Israel,
then when all is said and done,
we realize God's curse has come?

Could it be from great departure,
of Christians leaving in the Rapture?
Those left behind with little hope,
may lose their will to even cope?

Could it be from darkened sun
when ashes from volcanoes come,
and death to millions it will seize
who cannot find clean air to breathe?

tenth Sabbatical week of years completes a 490 year cycle, and the next year is a Jubilee year, which starts a new set of cycles.

Yom Kippur is celebrated by the Jews once each year as the Sabbath of Sabbaths. It is the holiest day of the year, referred to as the Day of Atonement, the Day of Reconciliation, and also the Day of Judgment.

Concurrent with Sabbatical years and weeks of years are Shemitah years and weeks of years. Thus, every seventh year and every 49th year and every 490th year are Shemitah years. All of those years end on Elul 29, the last day of the year on the Jewish calendar.

Our purpose for providing these details is to alert readers to the fact that the fall of 2015 will see the end of the *tenth* 490 year Shemitah and Sabbatical cycles.

The number "10" in God's numerology means "Divine Perfection," as in, the time has come, it's over. The specific closing dates are September 13, 2015, Elul 29, and September 23, 2015, Day of Atonement.

How much more evidence do we need that significant events are about to take place?

Well, we are just getting started, and here is where it really gets interesting!

We used biblical information to develop mathematical formulae to predict three very important upcoming prophetic fulfilments. All three fulfillments fall on a Day of Atonement, precisely, to the day.

The discoveries point to events in the near future that will be the most significant days in the history of mankind!

Those days predict the beginning of Daniel's seventieth week, great persecution of Christians, identification of the Antichrist, the Abomination of Desolation, the Rapture, the Great Tribulation, Armageddon, and the Second Coming of Jesus Christ to rule for a thousand years as a Righteous King.

The first date to watch:

The Day of Atonement, September 23, 2015. That date is exactly 17,640 days (49 years, a Jewish Sabbatical week of years) from June 7, 1967, when the Jews got full control of Jerusalem for the first time in nearly 1900 years.

Could it be from flood or fire
we lose our wealth and superpower,
or by quakes or storm or draught
that Mother Nature brings about?

Could it be from sky or sea,
a danger lurks that we don't see,
and by a bomb or meteor shower,
we lose our might in one brief hour?

For every mind that is discerning,
give attention to this warning:
the Court's attempt at Law annulment
will bring about God's certain judgment.

How would you interpret scripture
that gives a clear and vivid picture
of the ending of the Age,
and we're absent from the stage?

On the Feast of Trumpets, 2015, there will be a partial solar eclipse, and because the eclipse occurs on a Jewish holiday, it signals a warning to the world of an impending crisis.

If some significant event fulfills a prophecy, the connection would be hard to explain as *not* being orchestrated by God.

The second date to watch:

The Day of Atonement, October 2, 2017. That date is 25,200 days (a 70 year generation (70 x 360)) from October 4, 1948.

October 4, 1948, also was Tishri 1, New Year's Day, (Rosh Hashanah), and the Feast of Trumpets.

Earlier on May 14, 1948, Israel became a nation state. God waited until New Year's Day, in the fall to begin the countdown of the Final Generation so it would coordinate with the Day of Atonement exactly seventy years later, to the day.

Think about it!

The events we are witnessing, first hand, had to be orchestrated by a Supreme Being, who could see the end from the beginning, who was Omniscient, Omnipresent, and Omnipotent. Only the God who inspired their prophetic fulfillment qualifies.

In God's numerology the number "7" and its multiples mean completeness and perfection, both physically and spiritually.[15]

It was by Divine Plan that the Final Generation would begin on the first day of the seventh month on the biblical calendar, which also was New Year's Day on the civil calendar. And it was by Divine Plan that the generation would conclude on the holiest day of the year, the Day of Atonement, exactly seventy years later.

Thus, the countdown began on the first day of the seventh month of the same year the Jews were back in their Promised Land, and it ended in Divine Completion and Perfection on the Day of Atonement, a seventy-year generation later, to the day.

God often defined a generation as seventy years:

> The days of our years are threescore years and ten (seventy years), and if by reason of strength they be fourscore years (eighty years) *yet is their strength,*

That is the situation,
for America as a Nation,
and the scripture is precise
in its wisdom and advice.

But, our God we have deplored,
and His Word we have ignored.
Now there is a price to pay;
the time has come for judgment day.

Oh pleasure-driven "kingdom"
that brags of power and wisdom;
you've blasphemed and profaned
the God our founders claimed.

But, in a single hour,
you lose electric power.
You're in darkness and alone
and your sins are not atoned.

labor and sorrow (tribulation), for they are soon cut off (days are shortened), and we fly away (as in the Rapture). (Psalm 90:10, parentheticals are mine)

Jesus said:

This generation shall not pass, till all these things be fulfilled. (Matthew 24:34)

But more is involved here.

Likewise also as it was in the days of Lot; they did eat, they drank, they bought, they sold, they planted, they builded. *But the same day* that Lot went out of Sodom it rained fire and brimstone from heaven, and destroyed them all. *Even thus shall it be in the day when the Son of man is revealed.* (Luke 17:28-30)

The above Scripture implies that Christians will evacuate (be raptured) the same day America will be destroyed.

So let's look at that possibility.

The third date to watch:

The Day of Atonement, September 24, 2024. That date is exactly 2,550 days from September 22, 2017 (Tishri 1, 2017)

September 22, 2017 could be *extremely important,* because it is one of two upcoming days that qualify for the beginning of Daniel's seventieth week.

Here is why.

God declared through His prophet Daniel:

Seventy weeks are determined upon thy people and upon thy holy city. (Note: sixty-nine weeks of years have already passed, one week, seven years, remains to take place.)

191

In a flash of conflagration
fire destroys this mighty nation.
Millions die before its done,
when judgment for its sins have come.

Then, perhaps a moon eclipse
ushers in Apocalypse?
The flags of many ISIS forces
are colors of the rider's horses.

We're in the Final Generation;
the time has come for Tribulation.
There is no need for speculation;
the facts are there for observation.

Then you see the "Could it be's,"
progressing toward realities.
Who can argue, all is fine,
to fulfillments real time.

1. to finish the transgression
2. to make an end of sins
3. to make reconciliation for iniquity
4. to bring in everlasting righteousness.
5. to seal up the vision and prophecy
6. to anoint the most Holy. (Daniel 9:24)

According to NASA (National Aeronautical Space Administration),[16] there are eighty-six full moons from September 22, 2017 (Tishri 1, 2017) to September 14, 2024, (Tishri 1, 2024), which is precisely seven years or 2,520 days.

> And he (the Antichrist) shall confirm the covenant with many for one week (seven years on God's calendar). (Daniel 9:27, parentheticals are mine)

The verse above describes Daniel's seventieth week and the infamous Abomination of Desolation by the Antichrist.

The verse below describes the number of days to the consummation of the Age.

> From the time that the daily sacrifice shall be taken away, and the abomination that maketh desolate set up, *there shall be a thousand two hundred and ninety days*. (Daniel 12:11)

When we add 1,260 days (the first half) to 1,260 days (the second half) and thirty days, it becomes 2,550 days.

When 2,550 days are added to September 22, 2017, the date is precisely September 24, 2,024, which is the Day of Atonement, and the Day of Judgment, that wraps up the Age.

The key issue here is that only seven-year spans with 86 full moons qualify for Daniel's seventieth week, and there will not be another such span until September 2022.

If, in fact, Daniel's seventieth week begins *in 2017, then September 24, 2024 will be the monumental final Day of Atonement, ushering in the Day of the Lord!*

By the ruling of the Court
that inspired this brief report,
we continue in the sorrows
toward our future and tomorrows.

God is not amused,
when His laws we have abused,
and we are not excused
when His will we have refused.

If you have read these lines,
for you there still is time,
if you want to be acquitted
of the sins that you've committed.

Please don't wait another day.
find a place where you can pray.
Jesus loves you, as you are;
accept Him now, right where you are.

Arguments for Daniel's se^{ve}ntieth week to begin in 2017 include many significance additional events leading up to it:

1. The fact that the last of eight tetrads of lunar eclipses will end on September 28, 2015 (Sukkot), and it is the last tetrad of lunar eclipses on Jewish holy days for over 500 years into the future.

2. The fact that solar eclipses occurred on March 20th (Nisan 1, the first day of the biblical year) and on September 14, 2015, the first day of the civil year. Historically, solar eclipses have signaled imminent crises for the world.

3. The fact that September 14, 2015 is the Feast of Trumpets, and there will not be another Feast of Trumpets on a Jewish holiday within a Tetrad for over 500 years into the future.

4. The fact that September 13, 2015 (Elul 29) not only is the end of a Shemitah year of seven years, it also closes a forty-nine year Shemitah week of years and the *tenth* Divine Perfection, 490 cycle of Shemitah weeks of years,

5. The fact that the word "shortly" in Revelation 1:1 (King James Version) means, End-Time events will take place quickly once they begin.[17] World conditions tell us in unmistakable ways, those "events" have begun.

6. The fact that one of the mathematical formulae predicts the end of a seventy year generation, to the day, October 2, 2017, and that day is the Day of Atonement, the day of *completion* and *perfection*.

The end began with many sorrows;
it ends like Sodom and Gomorrah.
So why the need for more debates
on pre or post-trib Rapture dates?

On God's Word we can depend.
Are you ready to ascend?
We need not say, "the end is near"!
We now can say, "the end is here"!

Arguments for Daniel's seventieth week to begin in 2022 point to 2029 as the 2,000[th] anniversary year of the Crucifixion, which would close out 6,000 years since creation, ushering in seventh millennium, with accuracy. The argument is credible, if it was not for all of the converging *faith* to *fact* fulfillments that precede it, as we have just enumerated.

There is a caveat. At least one scholar thinks Jesus was born earlier than history records it.[18] If that is true, then history would have no competition as the year that begins Daniel's seventieth week.

We understand that the dates and other details in this chapter are numerous and probably difficult to absorb—perhaps even overwhelming. If that is the case for you, please use the information to guide your own study of the topic. There are many resources available on End-Time prophecy.

The reality of *faith* converging with *fact* in the fulfillment of so many age-old prophecies in the predicted generation, compels us to warn the world of the coming awesome Day of Lord with relentless fervor, courage, and uncompromising zeal.

An analogy expresses our position best.

Let's say I am a passenger in your car and you are the driver. I get a call on my cell phone and the person who called tells me there is a bridge out immediately ahead. Wouldn't it be my responsibility to warn you about that? That would be the most loving thing I could do at that point in time.

Well, the bridge is out, so to speak. But what lies ahead for individuals and America is far more threatening than two people in a speeding car approaching a missing bridge. And, the author of the warnings is God. *He promises not to confuse, and He does not lie!*

For all practical purposes, we no longer need to say, "the end is near"; we can say with confidence, "the end is here!"

Chapter 24

God Exists

There is a God, since time began,
who claims to be the Great I Am.
He is the cause of all we know;
from faith to fact, His Truth He shows.

There is a God of all creation,
whose language speaks to every nation.
The stars and planets in the sky
are silent signals from On High.

There is a God, down through the Ages,
who spoke His Truth through faithful Sages.
We know He's real through facts of proof
and by our faith that proves His Truth.

There is a God, whose Son was given
so we could live with Him in Heaven.
And for the time we dwell on earth,
His Plan includes our spirit's birth.

Jesus answered.... Before Abraham was, I Am. (John 8:58b)

And God said to Moses, I Am that I Am: and he said, Thus shall you say to the children of Israel, I Am has sent me to you. (Exodus 3:14)

In the beginning God created the heaven and the earth. (Genesis 1:1)

The heavens declare the glory of God; and the firmament sheweth his handiwork. Day unto day uttereth speech, and night unto night sheweth knowledge. There is no speech nor language, where their voice is not heard. (Psalm 19:1-3)

And God said, Let there be lights in the firmament of the heaven to divide the day from the night; and let them be for signs, and for seasons, and for days, and years. (Genesis 1:14)

Surely the Lord God will do nothing, but he revealeth his secret unto his servants the prophets. (Amos 3:7)

Now faith is the substance of things hoped for, the evidence of things not seen. For by it the elders obtained a good report. Through faith we understand that the worlds were framed by the word of God, so that things which are seen were not made of things which do appear. (Hebrews 11:1-3)

For God so loved the world, that he gave his only begotten Son, that whosoever believeth in him should not perish, but have everlasting life. (John 3:16)

[Jesus said]: That which is born of the flesh is flesh; and that which is born of the Spirit is spirit. Marvel not that I said unto thee, ye must be born again. (John 3:5-7)

Christ is God, who paid the price —
on the Cross, He gave His life.
As clouds grew dark and light diminished,
He breathed His last and cried: "It is finished"!

Christ is God, whose resurrection
conquered death for our salvation.
He's the One whose grace is seen,
teaching how to be redeemed.

Christ is God, who is the Way
to escape the fear of Judgment Day.
He's coming back to rapture all
who yielded to His Spirit's call.

Christ is God, who knows the ending,
from time that spans from its beginning.
It is through Him, all blessings flow;
it is through us, His Light must glow.

And he bearing his cross went forth into a place called the place of a skull, which is called in the Hebrew Golgotha: Where they crucified him.... (John 19:17-18a)

When Jesus therefore had received the vinegar, he said, It is finished: and he bowed his head, and gave up the ghost. (John 19:30)

He is not here: for he is risen, as he said. Come, see the place where the Lord lay. (Matthew 28:6)

For the grace of God that bringeth salvation hath appeared to all men, teaching us that, denying ungodliness and worldly lusts, we should live soberly, righteously, and godly, in this present world. (Titus 2:11-12)

Jesus saith unto him, I am the way, the truth, and the life: no man cometh unto the Father, but by me. (John 14:6)

I go to prepare a place for you. And if I go and prepare a place for you, I will come again, and receive you unto myself; that where I am, there ye may be also. (John 14:2b-3)

In the beginning was the Word, and the Word was with God, and the Word was God. (John 1:1)

Every good gift and every perfect gift is from above, and cometh down from the Father of lights, with whom is no variableness, neither shadow of turning. (James 1:17)

Let your light so shine before men, that they may see your good works, and glorify your Father which is in heaven. (Matthew 5:16)

The Holy Spirit, God's earthly agent—
always loving, always patient—
pleads for us to yield to Him;
repent of sin, believe in Him.

The Holy Spirit is God enthroned
in every heart that makes Him home.
No greater joy can we conceive
than peace that comes when we believe.

The Holy Spirit—God always present—
with strength for us to be resistant,
when Satan comes to temp or steal,
or make us doubt that God is real.

The Holy Spirit is God empowered
to help us share His Truth inspired,
and every Word of Truth we sew,
He multiplies and makes it grow.

And I will pray the Father, and he shall give you another Comforter, that he may abide with you forever. (John 14:16)

[Jesus said:] The time is fulfilled, and the kingdom of God is at hand: repent ye, and believe the gospel. (Mark 1:15)

Know you not that you are the temple of God, and that the Spirit of God dwells in you? (1 Corinthians 3:16)

Now may the God of hope fill you with all joy and peace in believing. (Romans 15:13)

Submit yourselves therefore to God. Resist the devil, and he will flee from you. (James 4:7)

Flee also youthful lusts: but follow righteousness, faith, charity, peace, with them that call on the Lord out of a pure heart. (2 Timothy 2:22a)

But ye shall receive power, after that the Holy Ghost is come upon you: and ye shall be witnesses unto me both in Jerusalem, and in all Judaea, and in Samaria, and unto the uttermost part of the earth. (Acts 1:8)

So also is my word. I send it out, and it always produces fruit. It shall accomplish all I want it to and prosper everywhere I send it. (Isaiah 55:11)

I have planted, Apollos watered; but God gave the increase. (1 Corinthians 3:6)

God is Father, Christ is Son,
the Holy Spirit make Three in One.
Emmanuel! God has come,
in Jesus Christ, His perfect Son.

He is Messiah, Anointed One.
Through Him alone is Heaven won.
No other god on earth can claim,
the power of prayer in Jesus Name.

Hallelujah! Praise His Name!
Eternal life is ours to claim.
How much we owe for all You've done,
and how we long for Your return.

The glory of Your majesty,
displayed in all of history,
through faith and fact, none can resist,
the marvelous Truth, our **God exists!**

For there are three that bear witness in heaven, the Father, the Word [Jesus], and the Holy Spirit: and these three are one. (1 John 5:7)

And they shall call his name Emmanuel, which being interpreted is, God with us. (Matthew 1:23)

But these have been recorded so that you may believe that Jesus is the Messiah, the Son of God, and so that through believing you may have life in his name. (John 20:31)

And whatsoever ye shall ask in my name, that will I do, that the Father may be glorified in the Son. (John 14:13-14)

And I heard as it were the voice of a great multitude, and as the voice of many waters, and as the voice of mighty thunderings, saying, Alleluia: for the Lord God omnipotent reigneth. By him therefore let us offer the sacrifice of praise to God continually, that is, the fruit of our lips giving thanks to his name. (Hebrews 13:15)

No good thing will he withhold from them that walk uprightly. (Psalm 84:11b)

And then shall they see the Son of man coming in a cloud with power and great glory. And when these things begin to come to pass, then look up, and lift up your heads; for your redemption draweth nigh. (Luke 21:27-28)

In this way God took away Satan's power to accuse you of sin, and God openly displayed to the whole world Christ's triumph at the cross where your sins were all taken away. (Colossians 2:15)

In the beginning God... (Genesis 1:1a)

Chapter 25

Thy Kingdom Come

*What excitement we are feeling
of all that God's revealing.
The timing of the dates,
He alone coordinates.*

*God knew of their beginning
and the timing of their ending.
Only now, they were discovered;
let their meanings be uncovered.*

*The stories once were mysteries;
now they're facts of history.
Once, no one could discern
the Truths now all can learn.*

*Bold colors, subtle hues,
paint pictures we can view;
fulfillment of the prophecies
are woven in the tapestry.*

In this chapter we express our imagination that highlights Jesus coming in the clouds in the Rapture and in the clouds at His second coming.

The focus of this book is on Jesus and our relationship with Him. The Bible provides hundreds of verses predicting His first and second comings. In our research, we discovered references that define important intervals of time, such that prophecies are made that specify beginning and ending points.

The fact that the fulfillments occurred exactly on the predicted dates not once, but several times, constitutes irrefutable evidence they were controlled by an intelligent Being who had the power and intelligence to make it happen. That Being could be only one Person, God!

We report many dates and times that connect important events with the present generation, even to the most likely spans of time when we can expect Jesus to come in the clouds, then later when he engages Satan and the Antichrist in the Battle of Armageddon.

Are you curious about the fact that many signs and signals and fulfilled prophecies have only recently been discovered? In fact, all of our discoveries were made since we started writing this book in 2012.

On the one hand, God exhorts us to "look up" (see Luke 21:28); He expects us to know the signs that signal His return. On the other hand, He tells us, "No one knows the day nor the hour" (see Matthew 24:36) of the Rapture.

It is a fact that nothing new has been added to the Bible, so the same Scriptures that helped us connect dates with End-Time events have been available to scholars and any other curious investigators for centuries.

We believe the reason the discoveries were made so recently resides in the fact that God Himself *"shut up the words, and sealed the book"*.

But thou, O Daniel, *shut up the words, and seal the book*, even to *the time of the end*: many shall *run to and fro, and knowledge shall be increased*. (Daniel 12:4)

I saw an angel in the sky,
at lightning speed, as he passed by.
I'm hearing now a trumpet blast,
by that angel who had passed.

I see a cloud of pure white,
and from it, beams of gleaming light.
What is the source? It is the Son;
for His Bride, He now has come.

In my vision, I could picture,
Christians caught up in the Rapture.
On the earth are open graves,
on the sea are troubled waves.

Riding on a beam of light,
each an instant in their flight,
at the time the call was given,
every saint left earth for Heaven.

The fact that the book is now open confirms the identity of *"the time of the end"*. The explosion of *transportation and knowledge* in this generation is a double, confirming witness along with all the other proofs of God's existence and End-Time revelations.

In Scripture Jesus is light, which illuminates, radiates, purges, and represents. He is both the source and its medium. No one can survive in His Presence without the transformational change that takes place at resurrection.

> We shall not all sleep, but we shall all be changed, in a moment, in the twinkling of an eye, *at the last trump: for the trumpet shall sound, and the dead shall be raised incorruptible, and we shall be changed.* For this corruptible must put on incorruption, and this mortal must put on immortality. So when this corruptible shall have put on incorruption, and this mortal shall have put on immortality, then shall be brought to pass the saying that is written, Death is swallowed up in victory. (1 Corinthians 15:51-54)

> For the Lord himself shall descend from heaven with a shout, with the voice of the archangel, and with *the trump of God:* and the dead in Christ shall rise first: then we which are alive and remain shall be caught up together with them in the clouds, to meet the Lord in the air: and so shall we ever be with the Lord. (1 Thessalonians 4:16-17)

> Then shall two be in the field; the one shall be taken, and the other left. Two women shall be grinding at the mill; the one shall be taken, and the other left. Watch therefore: for ye know not what hour your Lord doth come. (Matthew 24:38-40)

> And the sea gave up the dead which were in it. (Revelation 20:13a)

In the clouds where we have come,
angels welcome everyone.
Like sparkling diamonds are dew and mist,
and there is Jesus in their midst.

Millions in one massive throng,
begin to sing a choral song.
Oh, the beauty of the singing
through all of heaven ringing.

It's a song of invitation
to a glorious celebration.
At the marriage of the Lamb;
the Bride will join the Great I Am.

Oh, the glory of it all,
for those who hear the Savior's call.
In the twinkling of an eye,
we meet Jesus in the sky.

The Rapture of the Church could occur any day, but more importantly, it is set to occur under all reasonable circumstances within the lifetimes of most people now living. Because of that hope and expectation, it is *one of the most glorious times in all of history* to be alive.

What a tremendous honor to be among the living when Jesus Christ, our Savior, beckons His followers from a cloud, and saints, dead or alive, are resurrected into Heaven, to be with Him forever.

> And I heard as it were the voice of a great multitude, and as the voice of many waters, and as the voice of mighty thunderings, saying, Alleluia: for the Lord God omnipotent reigneth. (Revelation 19:6)

> Let us be glad and rejoice, and give honor to him: for the marriage of the Lamb is come, and his wife hath made herself ready. (Revelation 19:7)And to her was granted that she should be arrayed in fine linen, clean and white: for the fine linen is the righteousness of saints. (Revelation 19:8)

> And he saith unto me, Write, Blessed are they which are called unto the marriage supper of the Lamb. And he saith unto me, these are the true sayings of God. (Revelation 19:9)

> I Jesus have sent mine angel to testify unto you these things in the churches. I am the root and the off-spring of David, and the bright and morning star. (Revelation 22:16)

> And the Spirit and the bride say, Come. And let him that heareth say, Come. And let him that is athirst come. And whosoever will, let him take the water of life freely. (Revelation 22:17)

> He which testifieth these things saith, Surely I come quickly. Amen. Even so, come, Lord Jesus. (Revelation 22:20)

The beauty we are seeing,
are scenes from its beginning,
at the Supper celebration,
while on earth there's Tribulation.

Have your thoughts of what you've read,
changed your heart by what we've said?
Do the facts that you've received
cause your heart to now believe?

Will your lamp be burning bright,
so Christ can see its light?
Or does it even shine?
Will you be left behind?

How will those remaining here
overcome their natural fear?
What will be the heavy cost
of those the world will then have lost?

The Tribulation begins with the imposition of a counterfeit spirituality, presumed to bring all religions together in such an all-inclusive way that conflicts are resolved and worldwide peace and justice reign, as in a global utopia, or New World Order.

Three and one-half years into the Tribulation (Daniel's seventieth week), the Antichrist and His cohort, the False Prophet, break an agreement (covenant) they made earlier. That event (*hudna*) is marked by the construction of an image of the Antichrist, which is placed in the newly-erected temple in Jerusalem.

The Antichrist claims to be God and demands to be worshipped as such. Those actions introduce three and one-half years of the Great Tribulation, of such devastation and horror nothing like it has ever occurred in previous history, nor will it occur again.

> And he shall confirm the covenant with many for one week: and in the midst of the week he shall cause the sacrifice and the oblation to cease, and for the overspreading of abominations he shall make it desolate, even until the consummation, and that determined shall be poured upon the desolate. (Daniel 9:27)

> For then shall be great tribulation, such as was not since the beginning of the world to this time, no, nor ever shall be. (Matthew 24:21)

> And at that time shall Michael stand up, the great prince which standeth for the children of thy people: and there shall be a time of trouble, such as never was since there was a nation [even] to that same time: and at that time thy people shall be delivered, every one that shall be found written in the book. (Daniel 12:1)

213

Who will fill the empty shoes
of millions then the world will lose?
How will people then contain
all evil forces, unrestrained?

What is it you need to do—
your personal follow through—
to ensure your heart is right,
should the Rapture be tonight?

Do you believe that God exists,
and He grieves when you resist?
He wants to set you free,
when He says, "Come unto me".

If this message is for you,
you know what you should do:
seek a place of prayer;
God will meet you there.

Can you imagine the chaos that will take place when millions of people just vanish from the planet—selectively, that is only those who were known on earth as professing to be followers of Jesus Christ?

Clearly, many who are left behind will have claimed the same identity. However, God knows the difference between His true children and counterfeits and hypocrites—those who talked the talk but did not walk the walk.

The Holy Spirit empowered the Church at Pentecost. When He, as the Restrainer, leaves with the Church, the Antichrist will be released with power to perform his evil deeds.

> And when the day of Pentecost was fully come, they were all with one accord in one place. And suddenly there came a sound from heaven as of a rushing mighty wind, and it filled all the house where they were sitting. And there appeared unto them cloven tongues like as of fire, and it sat upon each of them. And they were all filled with the Holy Ghost.... (Acts 1:1-4a)

We believe the "restraints" are on the Antichrist until the Church leaves in the Rapture. However, the Holy Spirit continues to empower, because many will be saved through that power until Christ returns to earth at His second coming.

> And now ye know what withholdeth that he might be revealed in his time. (2 Thessalonians 2:6)

> For the mystery of iniquity doth already work: only he who now letteth will let, *until he be taken out of the way*. (2 Thessalonians 2:7)

> Come unto me, all ye that labor and are heavy laden, and I will give you rest. (Matthew 11:28)

Now, the vision we are seeing
changed the scene that we are viewing.
In the clouds, a glorious sight,
riding a horse of pure white.

The Son of God has come again,
and every eye is fixed on Him.
Across the sky at lightning speed,
riding hard on a gallant steed.

When He speaks, it's like a sword,
piercing, slashing every Word.
His Words and Presence are all He needs
to rid the world of evil deeds.

He engages the Beast and Dragon
in the Battle of Armageddon.
He wins the war, decisively,
fulfilling every prophecy.

Behold, he cometh with clouds; and every eye shall see him, and they *also* which pierced him: and all kindreds of the earth shall wail because of him. Even so, Amen. (Revelation 1:7)

And I saw heaven opened, and behold a white horse; and he that sat upon him was called Faithful and True, and in righteousness he doth judge and make war. (Revelation 19:11)

His eyes were as a flame of fire, and on his head were many crowns; and he had a name written, that no man knew, but he himself. (Revelation 19:12)

And he was clothed with a vesture dipped in blood: and his name is called The Word of God. (Revelation 19:13)

And the armies which were in heaven followed him upon white horses, clothed in fine linen, white and clean. (Revelation 19:14)

And out of his mouth goeth a sharp sword, that with it he should smite the nations: and he shall rule them with a rod of iron: and he treadeth the wine-press of the fierceness and wrath of Almighty God. (Revelation 19:15)

And I saw the beast, and the kings of the earth, and their armies, gathered together to make war against him that sat on the horse, and against his army. (Revelation 19:19)

And then shall that Wicked be revealed, whom *the Lord shall consume with the spirit of his mouth,* and shall destroy with the *brightness of his coming*: (2 Thessalonians 2:8)

The pictures in the tapestry
display the end of history.
His Kingdom truly will have come;
on earth, His will, will then be done.

For a thousand years He reigns,
putting ends to sin and shame.
He brings justice, peace, and one accord,
as King of Kings and Lord of Lords!

And the beast was taken, and with him the false prophet that wrought miracles before him, with which he deceived them that had received the mark of the beast, and them that worshipped his image. These both were cast alive into a lake of fire burning with brimstone. (Revelation 19:20)

And the remnant were slain with the sword of him that sat upon the horse, which sword proceeded out of his mouth: and all the fowls were filled with their flesh. (Revelation 19:21)

Then I saw an angel coming down from heaven, holding in his hand the key to the bottomless pit and a great chain. And he seized the dragon, that ancient serpent, who is the devil and Satan, and bound him for a thousand years, and threw him into the pit, and shut it and sealed it over him, so that he might not deceive the nations any longer, until the thousand years were ended. (Revelation 20:1-2)

They will make war on the Lamb, and the Lamb will conquer them, for he is Lord of lords and King of kings, and those with him are called and chosen and faithful". (Revelation 17:14)

Chapter 26

Thy Will be Done

In my ears I hear a song,
angels singing all day long.
The melody and words are clear;
they tell of love that casts out fear.

In my eyes I see the Cross
where Jesus gave His life for us.
That's why I now am free to claim
eternal life in Jesus name.

In my mind I think of God
and Truth that's written in His Word.
That Word is always Living Light;
it helps me choose each path that's right.

In my heart I feel compelled
to do and be what God has willed,
so every voice that speaks to me
brings more joy and love for Thee.

Then I looked and heard the voice of many angels . . . They encircled the throne and the living creatures and the elders. In a loud voice they sang: 'Worthy is the Lamb, who was slain, to receive power and wealth and wisdom and strength and honor and glory and praise!' Then I heard every creature in heaven and on earth and under the earth and on the sea, and all that is in them, singing: 'To Him who sits on the throne and to the Lamb be praise and honor and glory and power, for ever and ever!' (Revelation 5:11-13)

There is no fear in love; but perfect love casteth out fear: (1 John 5:18a)

For the message of the cross is foolishness to those who are perishing, but to us who are being saved it is the power of God. (1 Corinthians 1:18)

For this is the will of My Father, that everyone who beholds the Son and believes in Him will have eternal life, and I Myself will raise him up on the last day. (John 6:40)

Thy word is a lamp unto my feet, and a light unto my path. (Psalm 119:105)

But he that doeth truth cometh to the light, that his deeds may be made manifest, that they are wrought in God. (John 3:21)

Jesus said:

I am the Light of the world. So if you follow me, you won't be stumbling through the darkness, for living light will flood your path. (John 8: 12, TLB)

In my life Thy will be done
so on earth Thy Kingdom come.
In each life Thy Kingdom come
so on earth Thy will be done.

Our Father which art in heaven, Hallowed be thy name. *Thy kingdom come, Thy will be done* in earth, as it is in heaven. Give us this day our daily bread. And forgive us our debts, as we forgive our debtors. And lead us not into temptation, but deliver us from evil: For thine is the kingdom, and the power, and the glory, forever. Amen. (Matthew 6:9a-13)

Chapter 27

Introducing "Reflections"

This chapter highlights the *essence* of the information the book was written to convey.

First and foremost, of course, Jesus is revealed as the Son of Man and the Son of God, who offers eternal life as a free gift to all who believe in Him and receive Him as Savior and Lord.

While Christ's birth and life are facts of recorded history, His claim to be God, the second member of the Trinity, is a matter of *faith*.

Nevertheless, the factual evidence of His impact in the hearts and lives of true believers in the present generation and throughout history is irrefutable.

Also, the factual fulfillment of prophecies confirms, with certainty, God's existence. With that understanding, there are no excuses.

Every reader needs the assurance of sins forgiven. We provide a prayer for that to happen, and it will happen for those who pray the prayer with a sincere and contrite heart and have the *faith* to claim Christ's gift of eternal life.

In this generation atheists, false teachers, false prophets, and non-believers have gained respect in positions of authority, such that their message has had a significant deceptive influence. Important among their false teachings are:

1. There is no credible evidence that God exists.
2. Due to the absence of evidence of God's existence, the scientific method does not apply in tests that could answer the question and resolve the problem.

We challenged those claims and set out to examine the *problem* based on objective evidence.

The rationale for investigating these *issues* required data from fulfilled prophecies. While prophecies begin as *faith-based expectations*, when they are fulfilled, they become observable *facts*. Those *facts* can then be quantified and *scientifically* tested for cause-effect relationships.

Facts are plentiful from fulfilled prophecies regarding Israel's statehood and its subsequent growth and development. They clearly identify the present generation as the Final Generation, with all of the *tribulations* associated with it.

Fulfillments defined by that label take place every day, including increases in wars and rumors of wars, false teachers, and false prophets, the persecution of followers of Christ, natural disasters, and national alignments being positioned for prophetic wars, to name a few.

In addition to all of the above, cosmic activities since creation have signaled various crises to Jews and Gentiles. The convergence of fulfillments of those heavenly activities in the present generation is so important we report them in a sequel to this book, *Finding God through Science, From Fact to Faith.*

For people who continue to *believe* God does not exist, their *faith* is refuted by the facts.

The findings impose a heavy responsibility on the secular community. No longer will false teachers, atheists, and God haters be able to presume that all matter, human beings and all other forms of life came from nothing. Zero added to, subtracted from, multiplied or divided by zero, still produces zero. The only way nothing could become something is through the existence of an eternal, spiritual Being. That is what God claims to be, and His Word, our faith, and empirical facts of fulfilled prophecy all support that claim. To continue to disbelieve those observable realities is to deny documented truth and is intellectually dishonest.

Even more egregious are postulations that a *theory,* such as the Theory of Evolution, is *sufficient* as an interim explanation of the existence of all life forms, while continuing to search for evidence to support the claim. Wherever that occurs it is *not* science and the strategy should not to be dignified as an application of the scientific method.

Are you ready to meet God and to give an account of how you have lived your life? If not, don't put it off. The Bible is very clear; it says:

> For it is written, as I live, saith the Lord, every knee shall bow to me, and every tongue shall confess to God. (Romans 14:11)

Chapter 28

Reflections

*Here are our reflections
from a mirror of God's selections
of His promises and prophecies
which affirm His Word's veracity.*

*Prophecies for centuries sealed,
in our time, have been revealed.
The evidence is more than proof,
God's Word is Holy Truth.*

*The tests of faith's validity
are proof of God's reality,
in ways that give us confidence
God's Word equates to Providence!*

*That Word, of course, is our sword,
which we've gotten from the Lord.
Its two sharp edges we can wield
and faith is our protective shield.*

In this chapter, we selected Bible verses that represent the message the book conveys about Jesus, His Deity, His birth, life, death, resurrection, and ascension.

A major purpose of the book was to plant seeds of *truth* that encourage readers to seek Jesus, the only means by which they can obtain the gift of eternal life.

> In the beginning was the Word (Jesus), and the Word was with God, and the Word was God. The same was in the beginning with God. All things were made by him; and without him was not anything made that was made. In him was life; and the life was the light of men. And the light shineth in darkness; and the darkness comprehended it not. (John 1:1-5)

> He was in the world, and the world was made by him, and the world knew him not. He came unto his own, and his own received him not. But as many as received him, to them gave he power to become the sons of God, even to them that believe on his name. (John 1:10-12)

> But thou, O Daniel, shut up the words, and seal the book, even to the time of the end: many shall run to and fro, and knowledge shall be increased. (Daniel 12:4)

> Jesus said: "Now learn a parable of the fig tree; When his branch is yet tender, and putteth forth leaves, ye know that summer is nigh: So likewise ye, when ye shall see all these things, know that it is near, even at the doors. Verily I say unto you: This generation shall not pass, till all these things be fulfilled". (Matthew 24:32:34)

Faith and fact concur in Truth
that blesses us in daily use.
Its Light is with us every day,
which helps to keep us in the Way.

God the Father, Christ the Son,
the Holy Spirit, the Three in One.
All combine in Unity
as God in Holy Trinity.

Since God is always with us,
no weapon formed against us
can pierce our shield of faith
to harm a vital place.

So faith and fact converge,
and we're at the very verge
of leaving in the Rapture—
we're awaiting our departure.

For the word of God is quick, and powerful, and sharper than any two edged sword, piercing even to the dividing asunder of soul and spirit, and of the joints and marrow, and is a discerner of the thoughts and intents of the heart. (Hebrews 4:12)

Now faith is the substance of things hoped for, the evidence of things not seen. (Hebrews 11:1)

Faith cometh by hearing, and hearing by the word of God. (Romans 10:17)

Thy word is a lamp unto my feet, and a light unto my path. (Psalm 119:105)

For there are three that bear record in heaven, the Father, the Word [Jesus], and the Holy Ghost: and these three are one. (1 John 5:7)

No weapon that is formed against thee shall prosper; and every tongue that shall rise against thee in judgment thou shalt condemn. This is the heritage of the servants of the Lord, and their righteousness is of me, saith the Lord. (Isaiah 54:17)

Above all, taking the shield of faith, wherewith ye shall be able to quench all the fiery darts of the wicked. (Ephesians 6:16)

Jesus said: "Then shall two be in the field; the one shall be taken, and the other left. Two women shall be grinding at the mill; the one shall be taken, and the other left. Watch therefore: for ye know not what hour your Lord doth come". (Matthew 24:40-42)

And all of these reflections
are meant for our perfection.
Jesus Christ, the Son of God,
makes us perfect by His blood.

It cleanses seekers who believe
the Word of Truth that they receive.
He's hoping you will welcome Him
and by faith believe in Him.

He made a Way for your salvation,
by His life and crucifixion.
He's hoping you will welcome Him;
your sins were on the Cross with Him.

Jesus died in infamy
and rose again in victory.
He's hoping you will welcome Him;
your victory, too, is found in Him.

Be ye therefore perfect, even as your Father which is in heaven is perfect. (Matthew 5:48)

For by one offering he hath perfected forever them that are sanctified. Whereof the Holy Ghost also is a witness to us: for after that he had said before: This is the covenant that I will make with them after those days, saith the Lord, I will put my laws into their hearts, and in their minds will I write them; and their sins and iniquities will I remember no more. (Hebrews 10:14-17)

But God commended his love toward us, in that, while we were yet sinners, Christ died for us. Much more then, being now justified by his blood, we shall be saved from wrath through him. For if, when we were enemies, we were reconciled to God by the death of his Son, much more, being reconciled, we shall be saved by his life. (Romans 5:8-10)

And not only so, but we also joy in God through our Lord Jesus Christ, by whom we have now received the atonement. (Romans 5:11)

Who his own self bare our sins in his own body on the tree that we, being dead to sins, should live unto righteousness: by whose stripes ye were healed. (1 Peter 2:24)

He is despised and rejected of men; a man of sorrows, and acquainted with grief: and we hid as it were our faces from him; he was despised, and we esteemed him not. Surely he hath borne our griefs, and carried our sorrows: yet we did esteem him stricken, smitten of God, and afflicted. But he was wounded for our transgressions, he was bruised for our iniquities: the chastisement of our peace was upon him; and with his stripes we are healed. (Isaiah 53:3-5)

Fear not ye: For I know that ye seek Jesus, which was crucified. He is not here: for he is risen, as he said. (Matthew 28:5b-6a)

Without Him you are lost,
but for your sins, He paid the cost.
He's hoping you will welcome Him,
then live your life to honor Him.

He tells you that He loves you;
He's eager to forgive you.
He's hoping you will welcome Him;
please humbly give your life to Him.

Jesus has the power to save;
He left your sins back in the grave.
He's hoping you will welcome Him;
please open up your heart to Him.

He promised with your confession,
eternal life is your possession.
He's hoping you will welcome Him,
then trust, obey, and follow Him.

For the wages of sin is death; but the gift of God is eternal life through Jesus Christ our Lord. (Romans 6:23)

For God so loved the world that he gave his only begotten Son, that whosoever believes in him should not perish but have eternal life. For God did not send his Son into the world to condemn the world, but that the world through him might be saved. (John 3:16-17)

Neither is there salvation in any other: for there is none other name under heaven given among men, whereby we must be saved. (Acts 4:12)

Death is swallowed up in victory. O death, where is thy sting? O grave, where is thy victory? The sting of death is sin; and the strength of sin is the law. But thanks be to God, which giveth us the victory through our Lord Jesus Christ. (1 Corinthians 15:54-57)

If we confess our sins, he is faithful and just to forgive us our sins, and to cleanse us from all unrighteousness. (1 John 1:9)

If thou shalt confess with thy mouth the Lord Jesus, and shalt believe in thine heart that God hath raised him from the dead, thou shalt be saved. (Romans 10:9)

But be ye doers of the word, and not hearers only, deceiving your own selves. (James 1:22)

And he said to them all: If any man will come after me, let him deny himself, and take up his cross daily, and follow me. For whosoever will save his life shall lose it: but whosoever will lose his life for my sake, the same shall save it. (Luke 9:23-24)

He replaces sin and hate
with love and hope and faith.
He's hoping you will welcome Him;
He's calling you to come to Him.

He wants eternal life for you,
to be received through faith by you.
He's hoping you will welcome Him;
begin today your walk with Him.

When He comes He brings release;
how marvelous that sense of peace.
He's hoping you will welcome Him;
He'll fill your heart with joy in Him.

On your heart He gently knocks;
He waits to hear the latch unlock.
He's hoping you will welcome Him;
He wants you now to be with Him.

There are three things that remain—faith, hope, and love—and the greatest of these is love. (I Corinthians 13:13)

For by grace are ye saved through faith; and that not of yourselves: it is the gift of God: Not of works, lest any man should boast. (Ephesians 2:8-9)

The Lord is my shepherd; I shall not want. He maketh me to lie down in green pastures: he leadeth me beside the still waters. He restoreth my soul: he leadeth me in the paths of righteousness for his name's sake. Yea, though I walk through the valley of the shadow of death, I will fear no evil: for thou art with me; thy rod and thy staff they comfort me. Thou preparest a table before me in the presence of mine enemies: thou anointest my head with oil; my cup runneth over. Surely goodness and mercy shall follow me all the days of my life: and I will dwell in the house of the Lord forever. (Psalm 23:1-6)

Jesus said: "Peace I leave with you, my peace I give unto you: not as the world giveth, give I unto you. Let not your heart be troubled, neither let it be afraid". (John 14:27)

Jesus said: "Behold, I stand at the door, and knock: if any man hear my voice, and open the door, I will come in to him, and will sup [dine, fellowship] with him, and he with me". (Revelation 3:20)

People who have the capacity to think objectively and seek to know and understand the *truth* cannot deny that civilization is rapidly approaching an inevitable, catastrophic climax. That is such an obvious reality that neither this book nor any other is necessary for such a conclusion to be drawn.

Do I hear you softly praying?
Are these the words you're saying?
"I'm weary of my life of sin;
I want your peace and joy within.

My heart's door is wide open.
Jesus, you are welcome!
Make my heart your home;
let it be your throne.

Thank you for the price you paid.
Thank you for this prayer I prayed.
Thank you for the peace I feel.
Thank you for the gift that's real.

Yes, I do believe,
and yes, I do receive,
the Son of God today.
In Jesus' name I pray.
Amen!"

The signs are so apparent, their voice is clearly heard across nations, cultures, creeds, social classes, and political ideologies. Furthermore, from this point forward, the signs will not only continue but will become increasingly more frequent and recognizable. No application of human intellect or power can intervene to prevent the inevitable, approaching, global calamities.

This book makes every effort to alert people to their need of the Savior, whose free gift is eternal life and the only ultimate solution to mankind's sin-seeking nature.

In fact, if you have not already done so, this is another opportunity, right now, to face your personal spiritual condition and cry out to God for mercy.

For God says:

> Your cry came to me at a favorable time, when the doors of welcome were wide open. I helped you on a day when salvation was being offered. (2 Corinthians 6:2, TLB)

The *faith* to *fact, proofs* of *truth* reported here constitute what we believe to be an abundance of *necessary* and *sufficient factual evidence* to convince all open-minded readers about the reality of God's existence.

He waits to hear *your prayer,* when you unlock the door to *your heart,* and He will know when you sincerely do that. He longs to hear you say: *"Jesus you are welcome! I believe!"*

Chapter 29

Introducing "The Jesus Way"

There is a story that goes with this poem. It needs more commentary than others.

My very close friend, the late Jack Scharn, to whom this book is dedicated, wrote many poems. In fact, he published a book of poems.

I was intrigued by Jack's prolific ability to express himself through poetry. His poems told many fascinating stories, describing events from weddings, to babies, to nature and its beauty, to many wonderful years of a loving relationship with Aileen, his adoring wife.

While I enjoyed reading Jack's poetry very much, I never gave a thought to writing poems myself. Then one day, as I was praying, my words literally took on poetic rhyme and meter.

I was startled!

I rushed to tell my wife, Jan. She thought the words were interesting and encouraged me to see if the experience continued. Within a few hours, real time, this poem was written. My first. I was eighty years of age at the time.

Two years later, while spending some time in Sun River, Oregon, I wrote a second poem, then a third, and soon I was well along in writing what turned out to be this book.

Poetry forces the writer to articulate what is said in short, succinct, to-the-point verses. I find it to be an excellent medium for painting pictures in the mind, arousing curiosity, inspiring thought, and stirring the emotions.

With reference to the poetry here, I feel honored to believe and sincerely hope, I am merely the scribe—that these are *not* my words, but rather the inspired words of the Holy Spirit. Indeed, without that faith and confidence, the book never would have been written.

The experience has been an interesting one. Many times, the words required to express an appropriate thought simply were not there. At those times, when writing hit a wall, and I could not get through it, I prayed. The answer always came, and most of the time, quite quickly. The prayer broke the barrier, every time!

There is a promise that explains why God always answers those kinds of prayers: The need was "according to His will." God says in His Word:

Chapter 30

The Jesus Way

I'm walking with the Lord, talking to the Lord,
giving Him my thanks as I pray.
I'm listening to His voice, thinking on His Word,
looking to the Light that shows the Way.
This is the Jesus Way.

I'm seeking first His will, making sure He's heard
every need I have for the day.
I'm doing all I can to live His Truth and Creed,
loving everyone I meet today.
This is the Jesus Way.

I'm learning how to follow the call to be a servant,
treasures here on earth not to retain.
I'm resisting selfish greed by helping those in need
and finding secret joys that He sustains.
This is the Jesus Way.

I'm telling those I know that Jesus loves them so;
He gave His Holy life for all to save.
Then to the Cross we go to lay our burdens down;
a place where heavy hearts find true relief.
This is the Jesus Way.

The references for this chapter are relevant authorities to which the poetry points and no additional commentary is needed.

Pray without ceasing. In everything give thanks. (1 Thessalonians 5:17-18)

And your ears shall hear a word behind you, saying, this is the way, walk in it, when you turn to the right hand, and when you turn to the left. (Isaiah 30:21)

His delight is in the law of Lord and in His law doeth he meditate day and night. (Psalm 1:2)

Your word is a lamp to my feet and a light to my path. (Psalm 119:105)

Let your requests be made known to God. (Philippians 4:6)

Love your neighbor as yourself. (Mark 12:31)

And whosoever will be chief among you, let him be your servant... (Matthew 20:27)

Give to him that asks you. (Matthew 5:42)

You have made known to me the path of life; you will fill me with joy in your presence, with eternal pleasures at your right hand. (Psalm 16:11)

For God so loved the world that He gave His only begotten Son that whosoever believeth on Him should not perish but have everlasting life. (John 3:16)

Cast all your care upon him, for he cares for you. (1 Peter 5:7)

We overcome all sin through our trust in Him,
and that is why we sing our songs of praise.
So now our hope is sure, eternal life assured,
blessings far beyond what we deserve.
This is the Jesus Way.

We feel the Spirit's power, helping us endure,
making mountains flee into the sea.
God's grace and love invite you to give your heart to Jesus,
so you will have a peace not known before.
This is the Jesus Way.

When our journey ends, eternity begins.
We'll leave this world to go to Heaven's door.
There to hear the words: well done my faithful child;
you're home at last forever with the Lord.
This is the Jesus Way.

They triumphed over him [Satan] by the blood of the Lamb and the word of their testimony. (Revelation 12:11)

I will sing praise to my God as long as I live. (Psalm 104:33)

He does not treat us as our sins deserve or repay us according to our iniquities. (Psalm 103:10)

Not by might nor by power but by my Spirit says the Lord. (Zechariah 4:6)

Whosoever shall say unto this mountain, be thou removed, and be thou cast into the sea and shall not doubt…shall have whatsoever he says. (Mark 11:23)

For the grace of God that brings salvation hath appeared to all men. (Titus 2:11)

Peace I leave with you; my peace I give you… Let not your heart be troubled, neither let it be afraid. (John 14:27-28)

Well done, thou good and faithful servant… enter thou into the joy of thy lord. (Matthew 25:23)

Remarkably, today is July 24, 2015, the seventh month of the Gregorian year, and the twenty-fourth day of that month. Those facts cause me to call this the *eighth revelation*.

In God's numerology, the number "7" means "completion" and the number "8" indicates "a new beginning", both of which fit the situation.

We can test that hypothesis by observing what happens going forward. Several verses in Psalms 66 and 67, which represented *"My Call"*, Chapter 1, seem to apply now and in the future as fulfillments of the promises that would occur "in the end." Check those verses out and stay tuned.

Chapter 31

Survey: How Am I Doing?

———————————⌒⌒⌒———————————

On the next page is a brief survey to help you assess your relationship with God now, and periodically in the future. In the first four verses of the poem, *"The Jesus Way"*, there are fifteen action steps, where each action is introduced by the first person pronoun, "I". The context assumes you indeed are taking action steps expected of a believer, a follower of Jesus.

The survey provides an opportunity to examine your personal relationship with Christ. Its purpose is to help you discover your relative strengths and weaknesses so you know what to work on to improve. Thus, for every action step, ask yourself the question: *How am I doing?*

When you have finished the survey, add up the scores and do a self-evaluation of the results. However, don't feel guilty if your score is less than the perfect 150. Very few people, and probably no one, honestly deserves a perfect score; including myself, for sure.

Note your weaknesses and go to work on them. Do the following:

1. Find a time for daily devotions where you read your Bible and pray.
2. Diligently try to fulfill Jesus' exhortation in Matthew 6:33: "Seek ye first the kingdom of God and His righteousness."
3. Find a mature Christian friend to be a confidant, counselor, and mentor, and share your spiritual challenges in confidence.

4. Attend a Bible teaching church where you worship God consistently.
5. Join a small group Bible study for fellowship; try to grow in your knowledge of Jesus; let Him be your role model.

Allow a few months to pass, following your diligent effort to grow stronger in your walk with the Lord, then take the survey again. The survey is an attempt to help you be encouraged in your faith and to see objective improvement in your relationship with Jesus.

Survey

How Am I Doing?

INSTRUCTIONS: Photocopy this page. Then, in response to the question: *"How am I doing?*, mark each item 1 to 10, from "Sinner" to "Saint." Put your response on the line in front of each action step. Be brutely honest. Then later, improvements will register. You will be able to see your growth, and that will be an encouragement.

1. _____I'm walking with the Lord.

2. _____I'm talking to the Lord.

3. _____I'm giving Him my thanks as I pray.

4. _____I'm listening to His voice.

5. _____I'm thinking on His word.

6. _____I'm looking to the Light that shows the Way.

7. _____I'm seeking first His will.

8. _____I'm making sure He's heard every need I have for the day.

9. _____I'm doing all I can to live His Truth and Creed.

10. _____I'm loving everyone I meet today.

11. _____I'm learning how to follow the call to be a servant.

12. _____I'm resisting selfish greed.

13. _____I'm helping those in need.

14. _____I'm finding secret joys that He sustains.

15. _____I'm telling those I know that Jesus loves them so, He gave His Holy life for all to save.

16. _____My score is? Add the item scores to get your total score.

References

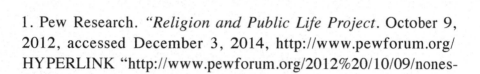

1. Pew Research. *"Religion and Public Life Project*. October 9, 2012, accessed December 3, 2014, http://www.pewforum.org/ HYPERLINK "http://www.pewforum.org/2012%20/10/09/nones-on-the-rise/"2012% 20/10/09/nones-on-the-rise/

2. Pew Research. Ibid.

3. Richard Dawkins. *"The Root of All Evil,"* The God Delusion," October 18, 2006 by Houghton Mifflin Co. (Boston/NY), 2006, accessed December 6, 2014, https://search.yahoo.com/yhs/search? hspart=Elex&hsimp=yhs-elex_v9p=The+God+Delusion&-type=normal

4. William Lane, Craig and Christopher Hitchens. *"Does God Exist,"* April, 2009, accessed December 6, 2014, https://search.yahoo.com/ yhs/ search;_ylt=AwrTccoTfoNUDcsAbJYPxQt.?p=Christopher+hitch-ens+science+and+God&fr2=sb-bot&hspart=SG Media&hs

5. Fulton Oursler. *The Greatest Story Ever Told*. Garden City, NY. Double-Day, Inc. 1949.

6. Reviewer. *The Greatest Story Ever Told*. Accessed July 24, 2015. http:// www.amazon.com/Greatest-Story-Ever-old/dp/038508028X/ref =la_ B001HCW61G_1_1?s=books&ie=UTF8&qid=1437773881&sr=1-1

7. Eric Metaxas. *Science Increasingly Makes the Case for God*. The Wall Street Journal. December 25, 201, accessed April 21, 2015, http://www.wsj.com/articles/eric-metaxas-science-increasingly-makes-the-case-for-god-1419544568

8. Eric Metaxas. *"Does Science Prove that God Exists"?* Fox Business. February 15, 2015, accessed April 21, 2015, http://video.fox business.com/v/3972101152001/does-science-prove-that-god-exists/? #sp=show-clips

9. Kenneth Taylor. The Living Bible Paraphrased. The Tyndale Publishing House, Wheaton, Illinois, 1972.

11. The Editors. *"Benjamin Netanyahu tells Europe's Jews to move to Israel, 'your home'"*. The Washington Times, February 16, 2015, accessed April 21, 2015, http://www.washingtontimes.com/news/2015/feb/16/benjamin-netanyahu-tells-europes-jews-to-move-to-i/

12. Mike Williamson. *SURE Technologies*. http://mikewilliamsonllc.com, 2015.

13. Editors. *Priestly Blessing*. Wikipedia Encyclopedia Accessed July 24, 2015, https://en.wikipedia.org/wiki/Priestly_ Blessing

14. *Elizabeth Howell. "How many galaxies are there"?* NASA, ESA, G. Illingworth, D. Magee, and P. Oesch (University of California, Santa Cruz), R. Bouwens (Leiden University), and the HUDF09 Team, April 1, 2014. Accessed April 23, 2015, http://www.space.com/25303-how-many-galaxies-are-in-the-universe. html

15. The Bible Study Site. *Meaning of Numbers in the Bible*. Accessed August 9, 2015, http://www.biblestudy.org/bibleref/meaning-of-numbers-in-bible/introduction. html

16. Fred Espenak and Alex Young. NASA Eclipse Website. National Aeronautics Space Administration, Last updated: April 11, 2014. Retrieved from http://eclipse.gsfc.nasa. gov/LEcat5/LEcatalog.html

17. Commentator. *A Simple, Face Value Understanding of Prophetic Scriptures*. Revelation Commentary. Retrieved from: http://www. revelationcommentary.org/01_chapter.html

18. Bill Heroman. *"Jesus Was Born in 7 B.C"*. NT/History Blog, Posted May 7, 2008. Accessed August 9, 2015, http://billheroman. com/2008/05/jesus-was-born-in-7-bc.html

CPSIA information can be obtained
at www.ICGtesting.com
Printed in the USA
FSOW04n1811191115
13633FS